Charles Darwin

mysterious islands.

Most remarkable was that Darwin did not yet know how important his stay in the Galapagos would be. Only later would he realize that these islands held the key to what he called "that mystery of mysteries—the first appearance of new beings on this earth."

On that September day, when Darwin and a landing party stepped ashore on Chatham Island, they were struck by its strangeness. They saw little that was green, except for stunted bushes and cactus. All around were black volcanic cones, like round chimneys 50 to 100 feet (15 to 30 m) high.

Galapagos Tortoises

The giant land tortoises of the Galapagos have a lifespan of 170 years or longer and can weigh up to 500 pounds (227 kg). Darwin sometimes took a wobbly ride on the back of a tortoise; the creature didn't mind, but the man had trouble staying on! Darwin also found turtle tasty. In fact, sailors captured so many for food that some subspecies became extinct. Today, the giant tortoises are protected in a wildlife sanctuary.

The islands had long been famous for their otherworldly landscape and wildlife, including the giant tortoises that roamed about. The Spanish had discovered the Galapagos in 1535 and called them *Las Encantadas*, the Bewitched, but they became better known by the old Spanish word for

Galapagos land iguanas can measure up to three feet (one meter) long, and males can weigh up to 29 pounds (13 kg).

tortoise—*galapago*.

The *Beagle* cruised among the sun-baked islands while FitzRoy drew his careful charts. Darwin collected as eagerly as ever, especially on James Island, where he studied the marine and the land iguana. Even with his great love of nature, Darwin did not care for the looks of the marine iguana. "It is a hideous-looking creature," he wrote, "of a dirty black colour, stupid and sluggish in its movements." Nevertheless, these ugly characters turned out to be the only seagoing lizards in the world! He watched hundreds of them thrash around in the shallow coastal waters, feed off the clumps of seaweed, then climb onto the black rocks to sun themselves.

The land iguanas were not any prettier, but they were different. Yellow and brown in color, they climbed the cactus plants to reach the newest, most tender growth. Like all of the Galapagos creatures, they were completely unafraid of humans. Darwin pulled the tail of one four-foot iguana, and it simply turned and stared at him. The birds, too, had no natural enemies and so had acquired no wariness of other creatures.

He saw other strange animals as well, such as a cormorant (shore bird) that could not fly, and penguins and seals—both cold-sea creatures—living in the tropical waters of the equator.

On October 20, Captain FitzRoy gave the order to set sail, this time homeward bound—a voyage that would take another year. On the deck of the *Beagle,* Darwin began to sort through his specimens, and he was struck by certain facts. First, he realized that he was looking at species that were endemic to the Galapagos—that is, they existed nowhere else. He had seen creatures in South America that were similar, but these on the islands were clearly separate species. On James Island he counted 26 species of land birds—all endemic. He wrote to Henslow, "I paid much attention to the Birds, which I suspect are very curious."

This Sally Lightfoot crab stares down a marine iguana. Adult crabs are brilliantly colored, while babies are black to blend in with lava rock.

What did it mean? Why were the birds and other creatures on the islands slightly different from those on the mainland? According to the Bible, God had created *all* the planet's creatures at the same time. If some species died out (and most people thought this was a big if), then God could have created new ones, but why would he create so many different species on these islands alone? What explanation could there be?

There was something else "very curious": The Galapagos Islands were only 50 to 60 miles apart, and yet the species varied from island to island. And later Darwin would remember a comment made by the vice-governor of the islands—that he could tell at a glance what island a tortoise was from by the markings on its shell.

Looking back, as the *Beagle* raced westward across the Pacific at 150 miles a day, Darwin realized with regret that he had not seen the significance of the vice-governor's comment.

There are 29 species of land birds and 19 species of sea birds in the Galapagos.

In his rush to collect, he had not bothered to note which island each specimen came

Red-breasted frigate

Blue-footed booby

Yellow warbler

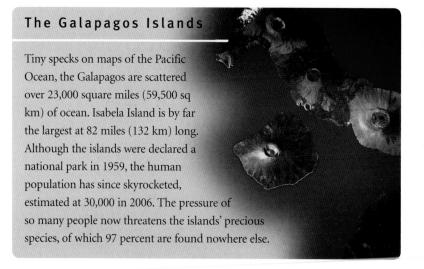

The Galapagos Islands

Tiny specks on maps of the Pacific Ocean, the Galapagos are scattered over 23,000 square miles (59,500 sq km) of ocean. Isabela Island is by far the largest at 82 miles (132 km) long. Although the islands were declared a national park in 1959, the human population has since skyrocketed, estimated at 30,000 in 2006. The pressure of so many people now threatens the islands' precious species, of which 97 percent are found nowhere else.

from. Now he could only wonder why the tortoise shells were different and why birds differed from island to island. "It is the fate of most voyagers," he later wrote, "no sooner to discover what is most interesting in any locality, than they are hurried from it."

On the homeward voyage, these impressions were only half-formed ideas—or, more accurately, half-formed questions. It was as though Darwin had been working on a large and complicated jigsaw puzzle by studying a few pieces at a time; then, after the Galapagos, he had a brief glimpse of what the entire puzzle would look like before it faded away again. Later, the questions—and the glimpse of the whole picture of evolution—would return to him again and again. That's why Darwin could write years later that his brief stay in the Galapagos was "the origin of all my views."

chapter 6

Home and a New Life

The voyage home from the Galapagos was relatively uneventful. After crossing the Pacific and Indian Oceans without any prolonged stops, though FitzRoy caused an irritating delay by crossing the Atlantic one more time so that he could double-check his Brazil charts. The men were furious and even the normally calm Darwin fumed, declaring, "I loathe, I abhor the sea and all ships which sail on it." Of course, he didn't mean it—he knew this had been the adventure of a lifetime.

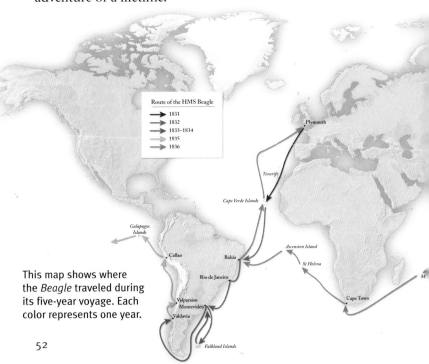

Route of the HMS Beagle
- 1831
- 1832
- 1833–1834
- 1835
- 1836

This map shows where the *Beagle* traveled during its five-year voyage. Each color represents one year.

Plymouth

Tenerife

Cape Verde Islands

Galapagos Islands

Callao

Bahia

Rio de Janeiro

Ascension Island

St Helena

Valparaiso
Montevideo

Valdavia

Cape Town

Falkland Islands

The detour to Brazil turned out to be brief, and the *Beagle* soon sailed north toward England. Finally, Darwin could write in his diary, "On the 2nd of October we made the shores of England; and at Falmouth I left the *Beagle*, having lived on board the good little vessel for nearly five years."

Darwin returned home a very different man. He was now nearly 26 years old, and his body and mind were toned by the weather and the adventurer's life. He dressed more like a sailor, in canvas pants and shirt, than a country gentleman. He had shown incredible endurance and courage on the ship and on land; he had made his way through encounters with wild animals, bandits, revolutions, and native war parties, not to mention hunger and thirst.

Darwin had also become a skilled scientist. He was dedicated to a careful gathering of facts, always totally absorbed in the problem at hand. In a letter to his sister Susan he wrote, "I literally could hardly sleep at night for thinking over a day's work." Combined with that devotion was a determination to understand. He constantly looked for a theory to explain what he observed. So far, however, he did not have a theory to explain the Galapagos. All he had were questions, and he knew he could not stop wondering about them until he found some answers.

os Keeling
Islands

Sydney

King
George's
Sound

Hobart   New Zealand

Scientific Curiousity

Public interest in learning about the natural world grew steadily during the 19th century. In Europe and North America, crowds flocked to displays of the skeletons of mastadons, saber-toothed tigers, and other extinct creatures. Archaeology became popular and amateurs pored over ancient ruins. Scientific lectures, given by societies like those Darwin that asked to speak about his work, were always crowded. The number of public museums multiplied—in one 20-year period, more than 100 museums opened in England. The U. S.'s Smithsonian Institution grew out of this urge to learn about the natural and man-made worlds.

One of Darwin's great surprises upon coming home was discovering that, thanks to Henslow, he was already a well-known and highly respected scientist. Sedgwick had also helped spread the word about Darwin's achievements. In a letter to Dr. Butler, Darwin's old headmaster in Shrewsbury, Sedgwick wrote: "He is doing admirable work in South America…and if God spares his life he will have a great name among the naturalists of Europe." Not surprisingly, the Geological Society and the Royal Society of London invited him to lecture, which he was pleased to do, although he suffered from severe stage fright.

These talks were a small part of the activity that made the two years following Darwin's return the busiest of his life. He had many books of notes and observations to organize, plus a diary of nearly 800 pages. There were mountains of specimens to go through, some that he had sent home to the Mount or to Henslow, and more crates still on the *Beagle*.

Darwin spent months rushing between the family home in Shrewsbury, and London and

Cambridge. He enlisted the aid of experts to help him sort, catalog, and analyze the specimens. Both Henslow and a new friend, the geologist Charles Lyell (whose book had inspired Darwin on the *Beagle*), offered constant encouragement and helped him get a government grant of 1,000 pounds to put together a five-volume study of the zoology, or animal life, of the voyage, which Darwin would edit. John Gould, a great ornithologist,

London's coal smoke and slum housing had multiplied during Darwin's absence.

would examine the bird specimens; and Richard Owen, a famous anatomist who studied the structure of living things, would take on the animals.

Darwin had to go to London so often the he finally decided to move there in 1837. He hated the city, calling it "dirty, odious London." Burning coal, both in fast-growing factories and at home, filled the air with soot, grit, gray smoke, and frequent dense fogs. But the city did give him a chance to dine with his brother, Ras, and with Lyell, and also to meet luminaries like math genius Charles Babbage and historian Thomas Carlyle.

About the time he made the move to London, Darwin received a surprising report from Gould, the ornithologist. Fourteen of the bird specimens from the Galapagos, Gould wrote, were mislabeled. The birds had looked so different from each other that Darwin thought he had collected finches, blackbirds, wrens, thrushes, mockingbirds, and others. Not so, Gould said. Of the 17 specimens, four were mockingbirds and 13 were finches. The finches had looked like different types of birds to Darwin because their beaks were so varied: One had a beak designed for seed

Gould's report on the Galapagos birds was key to Darwin's thinking. The ornithologist also had a special interest in hummingbirds.

Gould made this comparative sketch of four Galapagos finches, indicating that they might be of different species.

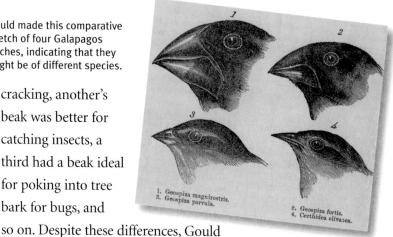

1. Geospiza magnirostris.
3. Geospiza parvula.
2. Geospiza fortis.
4. Certhidea olivasea.

cracking, another's beak was better for catching insects, a third had a beak ideal for poking into tree bark for bugs, and so on. Despite these differences, Gould explained, all 13 were finches; they were related to each other, but they were so unique as to be distinct species (in other words, they could not mate).

Gould's report put Darwin right back where he'd been as the *Beagle* left the Galapagos. He could no longer escape the idea that a single flock of finches from the mainland had made its way to the islands. Perhaps the birds had been blown there by a storm, some making it to one island, some to another. Over many generations, the original flock had slowly changed into 13 different species. He realized again what a huge mistake he'd made in not identifying the island from which each specimen had been taken. And he now suspected that the vice-governor's observation of different shell patterns on tortoises from different islands must be due to the same process of gradual change.

The logic of new idea was overpowering. A few weeks later, Owen offered strong confirmation based on his analysis of the

fossils Darwin had given him. All these extinct giant creatures, the anatomist said, were clearly related to similar but smaller

TRANSMUTATION

The term Darwin used to describe the slow change in species; the word used later was *evolution*.

creatures living today, such as armadillos, sloths, llamas, and others. Darwin realized that it didn't make sense to think that, after certain creatures had become extinct, God had decided to make new, slightly smaller versions of the same creatures. Instead, he now believed, older species had slowly changed into the creatures of today.

Ultimately, the finches and the fossils had convinced Darwin that species could change, or evolve. (In his notebooks and diaries from 1837 to 1838, he used the term *transmutation*.) But that still left a huge problem: How did these changes take place? How did a woodpecker come to use its beak as a powerful drill, for example? And how did a tree frog learn to climb trees? "I had always been struck by such adaptations," he wrote in his *Autobiography*, but "until these could be explained it seemed to me almost useless to [try] to prove by indirect evidence that species had been modified." Fortunately, he would not let the matter drop. Looking back on this period years later, he wrote,

Although his fossil analysis helped Darwin greatly, Owen later became envious, publicly smearing the famous scientist.

According to the Bible, God created all living creatures at the same time, as shown in this painting by Jacob Bouttats.

problem] about which I had long reflected, and never ceased working for the next 20 years."

In spite of his frenzied work pace, Darwin still had time to think about getting married. He was well aware of his brother's contented bachelorhood. Was that what he wanted, too? He carried on a curious debate with himself. He wrote notes to himself for and against getting married. In one column he wrote what marriage would involve; in the other, the results of remaining a bachelor. Written in late 1837 or early 1838, the sheet was titled, "This is the question."

If he married, he noted in the first column, there would be children and he would have a companion in old age, "an

children and he would have a companion in old age, "an object to be beloved and played with—better than a dog anyhow." There would also be the "charms of music and female chit-chat." These things, he noted, would be "good for one's health," but he would be "forced to visit and receive relations," resulting in a "terrible loss of time."

If he didn't marry, he jotted in the second column, he would have no companion. But he would have "freedom to go where [he] liked"

Darwin at age 31, a few months after his marriage to Emma, who was 30.

and to enjoy the "conversation of clever men at clubs." Also, he would not be forced to visit relatives or "to have the expense and anxiety of children."

He reached for a conclusion. Remaining unmarried, he decided, would mean "spending [his] whole life…working, working, working." Imagine, he told himself, "living all one's day solitarily in smoky dirty London House. Only picture to yourself a nice soft wife on a sofa with good fire, and books and music perhaps…Marry, Marry, Marry…."

Having reached this unromantic, scientific conclusion, Darwin now had to find the proper woman. When his cousin Emma Wedgwood came to London for a visit in the summer of 1838, Charles seized the opportunity. He proposed to her,

and they were married in January 1839.

Modern readers might find this courtship cold and unfeeling, but it was not unusual in the 19th century. At that time, the idea of marrying for love was not widely accepted and arranged marriages were still common. The idea was for a man and a woman to marry and then, hopefully, come to love one another. And, of course, Charles and Emma had grown up together, so they knew each other well. In addition, the numerous Darwin-Wedgwood pairings must have made the marriage seem quite comfortable.

Their life together proved that Charles and Emma were well suited and clearly loved each other. He needed someone to care for him without making many demands. Emma was happy to fill that need, according to the pattern of the times, and to be his companion, while also managing the house and overseeing the raising of the children. Emma's father, Josiah Wedgwood II, provided a bonus—a large sum of money which, combined with the amount Dr. Robert had already granted his son and Darwin's own sound investments, made the scientist far richer than he had thought possible.

Emma was excellent at archery, and had studied piano in Paris with Frédéric Chopin.

The Countryman's Doubts

The year 1839 was busy for Charles and Emma. They were adjusting to London, a city they both disliked, and their first child, William, was born. The other great event was the publication of Darwin's first book based on the *Beagle* journey, one in a three-volume set arranged by Captain FitzRoy.

Darwin waited anxiously to find out how his volume would be received, and was thrilled when he learned that readers were enthusiastic. He excitedly wrote to Henslow: "If I live to be eighty years old I shall not cease to marvel at finding myself an author." And, with characteristic generosity, he added: "This marvelous transformation I owe to you."

This photo of Darwin and his son was taken in 1842, when William was three years old.

Other publishing ventures were also underway, all based on the voyage. He was still editing and writing material for the five-volume zoology series, with major contributions from Gould, Owen, and other experts who had examined the specimens. And he had so much material on geology that he decided to write three volumes on that topic alone.

There was another writing project that no one knew about: Darwin could not stop jotting down notes on the problem of gradual change, or transmutation of species. Quietly, he began gathering information, searching for ways to fit the puzzle together. Without mentioning transmutation, he began writing letters to animal breeders, gardeners, zookeepers, and others to find out more about how species change. He knew that breeders could breed animals to promote certain traits, such as horses that were a little faster, cattle that were a little faster, cattle that produced better meat, or dogs that were better hunters or more gentle pets. Similarly, nursery owners bred plants for size, color, or other traits. He was hoping to find the process, or natural law, that would explain how and why these changes happened.

The Victorian Age

When Queen Victoria's reign began in 1837, the Industrial Revolution was rapidly transforming England. Cities were growing with incredible speed—crowded and dirty, but also lively and prosperous. Yet men still dominated society and government, and the monarchy strengthened tradition. In such fluid times, the queen stood as a symbol of stability, and her influence led to the 19th century being known as "the Victorian Age."

Darwin felt he could not tell anyone about this secret project, not even Henslow, Lyell, or Emma. The idea of transmutation of species was simply too revolutionary. To say

Galapagos finches were so crucial to Darwin's theory that today the islands' 13 species are known as "Darwin's finches."

that species changed over time would be much the same as saying the Bible's Book of Genesis was a myth. Darwin knew that people were not ready to hear anything so radical. Almost everyone accepted the Bible's account without question; at that time, the worlds of science and religion were in agreement.

Charles Darwin was understandably reluctant to defy this established order. But, as a scientist, he was a seeker of truth, determined to follow the evidence, wherever it led. Then, in late September 1838, he was reading a book by Thomas Malthus, a British clergyman and economist who was trying to understand the causes of suffering and death in the slums of London and other cities. In his 1798 book, *Essay on the Principle of Population,* Malthus pointed out that all species produced far more offspring than could possibly survive. If all the young of one species somehow survived, the planet would eventually be overrun by that species. This didn't happen, he argued, because populations grew faster than the available food supply, and in the struggle for that food, only a few survived long enough to reproduce. This provided a natural check on overpopulation.

Darwin agreed with Malthus's mathematics and quickly found new ways of applying them to the world of animals and

plants. He could see that some creatures had traits that made them better suited to survive. A deer that could run faster than others had a better chance of outrunning pursuers and surviving to have offspring. In turn, those offspring would continue to produce swifter deer. He could see this process most clearly in the beaks of the Galapagos finches. Some had beaks that were better for cracking open seeds, so they would survive on an island with lots of dropping fruit, while those with sharper pointed beaks would do best on an island with lots of insects to nibble. Creatures with such specialized features would survive in particular environments, while those without special survival traits would lose out in the competition for food and become extinct.

This was the process Darwin had been searching for. It was remarkably similar to the one used by plant and animal breeders. They decided on the traits they wanted and "selected" the

Thomas Malthus (1766–1834)

Malthus believed that human populations grew by geometric progression (4 to 8 to 16), but that food supply could increase only by arithmetic progression (4 to 5 to 6). Thus, it was futile to aid the poor— they would only have more children and double the starving. Malthus's influence caused England to pass a "Poor Law" in 1834, denying charity to people out of work. It took many years to replace this approach with more humanitarian policies.

particular plants or animals that would have offspring. For example, dachshund breeders began with a more standard dog. They selected the pups with the shortest legs and only allowed those to produce offspring. From those offspring, they again selected only the pups with the shortest legs to breed. After many generations, they finally produced animals with very short legs. This was "artificial selection." Darwin would call the same force in nature "natural selection."

He now had the essence of what would be his greatest contribution to science: a theory of how species evolved through the process of natural selection. In his autobiography he explained it this way: Because of the struggle to survive, "favourable variations would tend to be preserved and unfavourable ones to be destroyed.... The result of this would be the formation of new species. Here, then, I had at last got a theory by which to work."

Arriving at this point was more of a beginning than an end. Darwin still did not dare make his ideas public. He knew a theory must be tested by how well it explains a huge variety of facts—he had to gather more

Down House, in village of Downe, was the Darwins' home for 40 years.

The Darwin children found their father's study was always open if they needed a bandage, a spot of glue, or a hug.

evidence to make his theory ironclad. Only then would anyone accept it. The task of piling up evidence would continue for years. Fortunately, it was a task he loved.

As far as his family, friends, and the rest of the world knew, Darwin was deeply involved in writing about the *Beagle* voyage. By the time he had come up with his theory of natural selection in 1839 or 1840, he was also hard at work on a study of coral reefs.

His relationship with Emma continued to deepen, and he was thrilled to be a father. He spent hours playing with William and their second child, Annie. After her arrival, the need for a larger house became urgent. In late 1842, the Darwins bought Down House, less than 20 miles outside London.

Both Charles and Emma were delighted with their new home and happy to be back among farms and fields. Over the next 14 years, eight more children were born at Down House, three girls and five boys. Luckily, Down House was plenty large enough for the growing family and the large staff of

servants. Darwin selected one large room for his study, filling it with books, stacks of notes and correspondence, boxes, jars and bottles of specimens, and assorted stuffed birds.

Life quickly settled into a pleasant pattern, which remained little changed for the next 40 years. Darwin's relationship with his children was always loving and filled with fun. A daughter recalled: "To all of us he was the most delightful play-fellow."

A typical day began with a stroll on a path called the Sandwalk, which Darwin had constructed on the grounds. "The Sand-walk was our play-ground as children," his son remembered, "and here we continually saw my father as he walked around. He liked to see what we were doing." Breakfast was at 8:00 a.m., followed by an hour or two of writing. Then Darwin read the morning mail, did more work, took another stroll, and sometimes had a cold outdoor shower, which he thought was good for his health.

After the midday meal, Darwin read newspapers and wrote correspondence. He rested for an hour, often with Emma reading to him from a novel. In the late afternoon, he sometimes wrote or worked on experiments, often with the children pitching in. Supper was a light meal and afterward he liked to play backgammon. He once told a friend, with his typical attention to detail, that he had won 2,795 games of backgammon and Emma had won 2,490. Darwin then read a science book for a bit and was in bed by 10:30 p.m.

This routine would probably be too monotonous for many people, but such was the regulated life of a man

dedicated to scientific inquiry. And the routine was often interrupted by short excursions, or visits from family or friends. There is also every indication that Emma enjoyed their lifestyle as much as Charles did. "She has been my greatest blessing," he wrote of her, "and I can declare that in my whole life I have never heard her utter one word I would rather have been unsaid."

Yet as Darwin was settling into his life at Down House, not quite everything was perfect. He began to suffer a serious and permanent breakdown of his health, and was stricken with a variety of painful and disabling symptoms. In a life of such apparent peace and contentment, what was causing such strange ailments? Was there a connection between his illness and his secret theory?

For Darwin, every stroll on the Sandwalk was an excursion into the natural world.

8

Health Matters

In the years following the move to Down House, Darwin's reputation grew steadily. In 1842, his first book of geology was published on the subject of coral reefs. Darwin showed that coral reefs were created by tiny marine creatures, which required warm, shallow water. As new colonies of coral grew on top of the old, the older colonies gradually sank, forming rings, or atolls. These reefs, he explained, were alive only at the very top; they were dead at the bottom, and grew very slowly over thousands of years. He was relieved and thrilled that his good friend Charles Lyell was enthusiastic about the idea, since it contradicted some of Lyell's own work.

Two more geology volumes, on volcanic islands and South America, were already underway. In addition, his five-book series on zoology was completed in 1843, and his volume in the three-part *Voyage of the Beagle* continued to be popular. Although Darwin still did not dare to tell anyone about his theory of evolution, his literary output

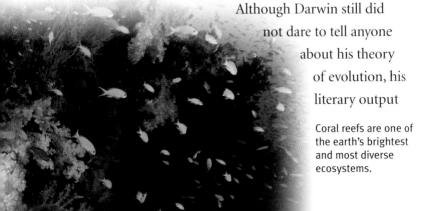

Coral reefs are one of the earth's brightest and most diverse ecosystems.

had still been astounding.
It's interesting to think
of this dedicated scientist
carefully filling his pages day
after day—not only writing
longhand, but doing so with
a quill dipped in an inkwell
or bottle. (The invention
of the typewriter and the
fountain pen were still
several years away.)

It was in the midst of this
creative and rewarding time
that Darwin's health broke
down. Apparently without
warning, he would be struck
with excruciating headaches,
often accompanied by
prolonged vomiting. The
symptoms varied with each
episode, and might involve
pains around the heart,

Sir Charles Lyell (1797–1875)

Few people had a more powerful influence on Darwin's thinking than Sir Charles Lyell. This was especially true during the *Beagle* years, when Darwin was developing his observation and recording skills. Lyell's *Principles of Geology* helped him see that changes in the earth happened slowly over time. This made the next step easier—that is, to deduce that life-forms also emerged through gradual change.

stomach cramps, trembling, painful skin rashes, and a general
feeling of weakness. The duration of the episodes varied, but
some laid him low for days.

The family traveled less frequently, and fewer people were
invited to visit. Darwin even had a mirror installed outside

Down House so that he could see who was coming and avoid those who would exhaust him. The man who had been such a vigorous adventurer had become an invalid, suffering from a chronic ailment that no one seemed able to diagnose. He was understandably discouraged by these bouts of illness, and wrote: "It has been a bitter mortification for me to digest the conclusion that 'the race is for the strong,' and that I shall probably do little more, but be content to admire the studies others make in science."

What caused Darwin's health to break down so completely? Using his own description of his symptoms, historians and specialists have come up with several different diagnoses. Some psychiatrists suggest that the illness was psychosomatic—meaning that Darwin experienced very real physical symptoms brought on by psychological factors, such as stress, anxiety, or repressed grief. They consider the illness to be the result of stress: his initial breakdown coincided with his first work—and secrecy—concerning evolution. His anxiety then showed itself through stomach pains, vomiting, and other symptoms.

Bugs of the *Triatominae* family cause Chagas's disease, which is still prevalent in poor areas of Central and South America.

Other specialists agree that the illness was psychosomatic, but they see the original cause in Darwin's family history. One popular theory is that eight-year-old Charles had been unable to grieve over the death of his mother. His long-repressed anguish finally emerged as physical illness. A less-popular theory is that his childhood dread of his domineering father triggered the outbreak of symptoms.

Could Darwin have had a purely physical illness? Some of the symptoms, like heart palpitations, had emerged during earlier periods of stress on the *Beagle*. During this time Darwin could also have been exposed to Chagas's disease. Throughout his travels in the tropics, he grew accustomed to awakening in the morning covered with flea bites. On one night he suffered what he called an "attack of the Benchuga"— an ugly little bloodsucking insect. Darwin caught one of the bugs and let it perch on his finger. "The bold insect," he wrote, "would immediately protrude its sucker, make a charge . . . and draw blood." This insect is now known to cause Chagas's disease, which causes a high fever and attacks the liver and other organs. Could such a disease produce symptoms over a span of some forty years? Such a prolonged effect is very unlikely, but not impossible.

Finally, there is the possibility that the illness was both physical and psychological. Perhaps elements of Chagas's disease remained dormant until triggered again by stress or anxiety. But whatever the cause of Darwin's suffering, he was clearly in a great deal of pain. His butler recalled, "Many a time when I was helping to nurse him, I've thought he would die in my arms."

"Gleams of Light"

I n spite of the almost-daily pain and discomfort, Darwin continued to work secretly on gathering evidence to support his theory of evolution through natural selection. In 1842, he wrote a 35-page summary of his ideas, titled "Sketch," followed two years later by an expanded version, called "Essay."

Although he was still not ready to go public, Darwin gave the longer essay to Emma with instructions to have it published if he should die suddenly. She probably did not read the 230-page manuscript because she was not interested in the details of his work. She knew only that he was working secretly on what she called his "discoveries."

Another event in 1844 made him even more reluctant to publish his theory. A Scottish writer and bookseller named Robert Chambers published a book titled *Vestiges of the Natural History of Creation*. Offering almost no evidence to support his theory and no explanation of how changes happened, Chambers simply stated that all species of plants and animals had evolved slowly over time, following certain natural laws, rather than being created by God.

Readers, including scientists, found the claims wild and improbable. Chambers may have suspected such a reaction, so he published *Vestiges* anonymously. Darwin was surprised by

how strong the outcry was. After all, the idea of evolution was not really new. His grandfather Erasmus had written about it a half-century earlier, and a number of scholars had suggested the possibility. Apparently people were shocked that someone would present it as established fact, especially with no proof.

For Darwin, the outrage over *Vestiges* confirmed his feeling that he was not ready to publish. It was clear now that the public, especially scientists, would insist that any new idea, or theory, must be supported by powerful evidence. He was confident that both his theory of evolution and the process of natural selection were right. But he felt he needed time to gather even more evidence; he wanted the proof to be so overwhelming that every possible objection would be answered.

Another reason for his reluctance to publish was that he didn't want to endanger his position in England's privileged class. What would happen if he and his family became social outcasts because of the dispute? He would lose his special position among the respected leaders of English society.

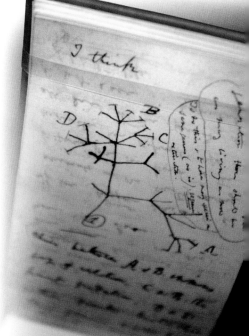

Darwin's 1837 drawing of an evolutionary tree was the first of its kind. He titled it with the striking note, "I think."

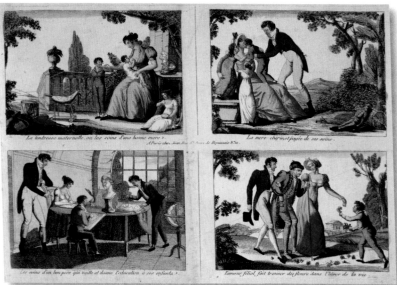

La tendresse maternelle, ou les soins d'une bonne mère.
A Paris chez Jean Jean St Jean de Beauvais N°20.

La mère chérie et payée de ses soins.

Les soins d'un bon père qui veille et donne l'éducation à ses enfants.

L'amour filial fait trouver des fleurs dans l'hiver de la vie.

It was very important to Darwin to maintain a comfortable life in which he could pursue his own interests, supported by the Down House staff (which included a butler, a footman, two gardeners, a cook, and several maids, as well as a nurse for the children).

Darwin was afraid to compromise the calm and rewarding life of an upper-class 19th-century family.

And then there was his concern for Emma. They were very close and he didn't want to cause her pain. He knew that his theory would unleash a storm of religious debate, which would be very hard for Emma. She was a devout Unitarian and she had worried for years about Charles's lack of religious conviction. Emma was certain that entry into heaven was reserved for those who accepted what was called the "Christian Revelation"—Christ's offer of eternal life. In

a touching letter to him, she expressed her great fear that they might not be together in heaven:

"Everything that concerns you concerns me," she wrote, "and I should be most unhappy if I thought we did not belong to each other forever."

Darwin's own religious beliefs had been weakening for several years. While first developing his theory, Darwin still believed in God, but in time he became an agnostic. He admired the practice of Christianity, but understood that there was inevitable conflict between evolution and a literal interpretation of the Bible, especially the Book of Genesis, with its story of creation taking place in only a few days.

In 1851, the last remnants of his more conventional beliefs disappeared, when his oldest daughter Annie died

Darwin was thrilled by the completion of his greenhouse. Today, botanist and historian David Kohn recreates some of Darwin's experiments in it.

of tuberculosis at the age of 10. By all accounts she was an exceptional child, and he was devastated by her death. It was common in Victorian England for a parent to write a semiprivate "memorial" of a deceased child. One week after Annie's death, Darwin described her personality in this memorial: "Her joyousness and animal spirits radiated from her whole countenance and rendered every movement elastic and full of life and vigour.... She was very popular in the whole household, and strangers liked her and soon appreciated her. The very manner in which she shook hands...showed her cordiality."

Because Darwin worked at home, surrounded by his family, his work on nature could hardly be separated from

the human nature he lived with daily. His grief over his daughter came just three years after his father's death. These two losses changed his ideas of both religion and evolution. In light of the pain

The death of his beloved Annie tormented Darwin, who feared he had passed his susceptibility to illness on to his children.

and suffering he had experienced, as well as all that he had seen in the world, he could not accept the image of a benevolent (kindly) God. And he rejected his era's belief that God made humans suffer as a way for them to grow morally. What about all the animals in the world? Animals, he wrote, "often suffer greatly without any moral improvement." But gradually his pessimism was softened by his usual love of life.

Annie's Box

Darwin's great-great-grandson inherited Annie's writing box and its contents. Inside, Emma had tucked her husband's memorial and his daily notes on the progression of her illness. Darwin is sometimes thought of as an unemotional scientist, but his great love and grief show otherwise.

Throughout the 1840s and 1850s, Darwin continued to add to the evidence supporting evolution, which he now referred to as "my theory." After writing his 1844 "Essay," he began to wonder to whom he might show it for their reaction. He settled on one of his newest friends, a young botanist named Joseph Hooker. Hooker and Lyell were among the few scientists who were welcome visitors at Down House.

To introduce Hooker to his revolutionary theory, Darwin

> *"At last gleams of light have come and I am almost convinced that species are not immutable.... I think I have found out the simply way species become exquisitely adapted to various ends."*
>
> –Darwin, in his letter to Hooker

wrote him a letter filled with very broad hints: "I have been now ever since my return [from the voyage] engaged in a very presumptuous work, and I know no one...who would not say a very foolish one. I was so struck by the distribution of the Galapagos organisms etc. etc....that I determined to collect blindly every sort of fact, which could bear in any way on what are species.... At last gleams of light have come and I am almost convinced (quite contrary to the opinion I started with) that species are not (it is like confessing a murder) immutable [unchangeable].... I think I have found out (here's presumption!) the simple way species become exquisitely adapted to various ends."

Hooker must have been stunned by the letter, which to a mid-19th-century Englishman, even a scientist, must indeed have seemed like "confessing a murder." The very idea that species could, and did, change, was an intellectual, emotional,

CONTROVERSY

A public argument between groups that hold opposing views on an issue.

and psychological shock that upset all conventional thinking about the origins of life. It would not have been much more shocking if Darwin claimed to have proof that the earth was flat.

Later, Darwin sent his "Essay" to Hooker, who still was not convinced by the longer explanation of evolution and natural selection. But he had confidence in Darwin, so he traveled to Down House, and the two brilliant naturalists had several long talks as they strolled over the Sandwalk. Finally, Hooker accepted that his friend had discovered an extraordinary truth. But he also knew the theory was explosive and would create enormous controversy. Nevertheless, he urged Darwin to continue adding evidence and preparing a manuscript for publication. By now, a full ten years had passed since Darwin started his first notebook on evolution. With the support of another scientist, was it finally time to go public?

Sir Joseph Hooker, (1817–1911)

Early in his career, Joseph Hooker wanted to travel to distant parts of the world—which was very unusual in his time. Still, he made scientific explorations in Antarctica, the Himalayas, and the Rocky Mountains. Hooker became a great botanist, and wrote numerous publications. Like his father, he also became Director of the Royal Botanic Gardens at Kew.

chapter **10**

Delay . . . and Completion

Imagine holding onto a great secret—maybe an invention or discovery. You know it could make you famous and you're eager to let the world know. But you're afraid. What if your secret makes everyone furious?

That's the dilemma Charles Darwin now faced. And how did he resolve it? Despite Hooker's newfound support, he did what most of us would have done: He delayed.

First, he was haunted by all those fears of disrupting family life and stirring up trouble. But there were other reasons for putting it off. For one thing, he was determined to be thorough. He felt that there were questions about evolution for which he still had no answers, such as how species could spread to remote parts of the world and then change, or evolve. He was also trying to develop a detailed study in biology.

Darwin chose to study barnacles—the little, hard-shelled, ocean-dwelling crustaceans that form colonies on rocks and other underwater surfaces, including the undersides of ships. He had decided to do the study at the urging of Hooker, who pointed out that it would strengthen his reputation as a scientist, thus making his theory more respectable. Darwin already had lots of information on barnacles from the *Beagle* voyage, and he thought he could complete the book in a few months and then give evolution his full attention.

In his usual drive to be relentlessly complete, however, Darwin piled up enough material not just for one book, but four, and the project chewed up more and more time. For eight years, from 1846 to 1854, most of his time was devoted to barnacles, interrupted by family matters and by bouts of illness. The last four of the Darwin's children were also born during this stretch of time, and the little ones often observed him in his study. In later years, the family enjoyed telling the story of the children asking friends, "And where does *your* father work on his barnacles?"

Darwin sometimes referred to the creatures as "my beloved barnacles." But the study wore him out! Near the end, he wrote to his cousin William Darwin Fox, "I hate a barnacle as no man ever did before, not even a sailor on a slow-moving ship."

Although the barnacle study did not figure directly in his theory of evolution,

This page from Darwin's study shows various barnacles. Today there are about 1,220 known species.

Thomas H. Huxley
(1825–1895)

Like Darwin, Huxley gained fame by dispatching scientific reports from an around-the-world voyage. Although he was only 25 years old when he returned, leading scientists were eager to meet him. Huxley wrote authoritatively on many subjects and was an outstanding speaker. As the most vocal supporter of Darwin's work, he became known as "Darwin's bulldog."

the work did have value. It showed that Darwin was a well-trained naturalist, and added to his stature in the scientific community. Hooker was enthusiastic about it, and so was a new friend, Thomas H. Huxley, a young zoologist. In a letter to Darwin's son Francis, Huxley wrote that Darwin "never did a wiser thing than when he devoted himself to the years of patient toil which the [barnacle] book cost him." This rigorous study also allowed Darwin to approach evolution with knowledge of anatomy and taxonomy (the classification of plants and animals).

Throughout his eight years of labor, Darwin never stopped gathering evidence on evolution— and work sped up after the barnacle books were published in 1854. For example, he continued trying to find out how different species were spread across different parts of the world. He was particularly interested in how species reached remote islands, which had

a high percentage of endemic species (that is, species found nowhere else). He questioned hunters, sailors, ornithologists, and others about how far birds could fly and where their migration routes were located.

Darwin hypothesized that seeds, if they could survive in salt water, could drift over hundreds of miles of ocean. Then, after the seeds germinated, or sprouted, on a remote island such as one of the Galapagos, the plants would slowly evolve in order to meet the challenges of the new environment. In a letter to Hooker in 1855, he wrote with typical enthusiasm: "I have in small bottles out of doors, exposed to variation of temperature, [water]cress, radish, cabbages, lettuces, carrots, and celery, and onion seed. These, after immersion [in salt water] for exactly one week, have all germinated, which I did not in the least expect." He even managed to demonstrate that seeds stuck to the mud on birds' feet could be carried long distances and still germinate.

Pigeon breeding was a nationwide craze in the mid-19th century. The birds were raised for shows, races, and to carry messages over long distances.

The Darwin children loved helping with their father's experiments, and, from 1839 to 1856, there was always at least one child under school age at Down House. They were willing participants when Charles decided to breed pigeons to see how artificial selection led to birds with certain traits. They also eagerly kept his seedlings damp, moved jars in and out of the sunlight, and joined their father on visits to plant and animal breeders. And, for his part, no matter how hard he worked, Darwin seemed willing to drop everything to join their games or tell them stories.

In 1856, he finally felt he had enough evidence to prepare his great theory for publication. He planned to title the book *Natural Selection* and, as usual, the pages started to pile up. Hooker, Lyell, and Huxley urged him to move faster. Time seemed to be racing by and they were understandably worried that some other ambitious scientist would beat him to it.

His friends were keenly aware of how rapidly England—and the whole civilized world—was changing in the mid-19th century. Much of this change was initiated by advances in science and technology. The spread of railroads and steamships, the development of new machines for agriculture and industry, and the rise in innovations like photography showed that England and the West were entering an exciting era.

An event that symbolized the new age of change had begun in May 1851, when Queen Victoria presided over the opening of the Great Exhibition. For six months, thousands of visitors trooped through the awesome Crystal Palace. While exhibits came from all over the world, visitors were most impressed by the scientific and industrial progress achieved by England and the United States: mechanical devices such as sewing machines, a high-speed printing press, and machines used to make tools.

People felt they were living in a world of wonders.

The changes in the physical world were accompanied by a new mood of acceptance for inventions and ideas. The subject of evolution, for example, was no longer taboo. Robert Chambers's book, *Vestiges of Creation,* had even been reissued and was taken more seriously than it had been a decade earlier.

Early in 1858, Darwin had about 10 chapters of *Natural Selection* written, but he still had a long way to go. It was at this point that he received a terrible shock—one that threatened to destroy his grand dream of presenting a major scientific discovery.

The Crystal Palace was a wonderous sight, built with 5,000 iron girders and 30,000 panes of glass.

chapter **11**

Going Public

On the morning of June 18, 1858, Darwin was strolling along the Sandwalk when a servant brought him a package from a young naturalist named Alfred Russel Wallace. Sent from a tropical island in what is now Indonesia, the package contained a letter from Wallace and a draft of an essay. Would Darwin be so kind as to read the essay, send it on to Lyell, and then see if it could be published?

Darwin opened the package and began reading. He stopped abruptly, gasping, his heart pounding. What was this? His hands trembled and he felt faint as he continued reading with increasing horror. The essay was a perfect summary of his theory of evolution!

He could hardly believe it. "If Wallace had my [1842 sketch]," Darwin wrote, "he could not have made a better short abstract! Even his terms [could be] heads of my chapters." Darwin had been scooped, just as his friends had warned. Wallace had even come up with the idea of natural selection (although without naming it), and, like Darwin, had arrived at it by reading Malthus's book on population.

SCOOPED

A person or publication is scooped when a rival is first to make an important story public.

Darwin was in despair. All those years of effort had been wasted! But Lyell and Hooker refused to give up. They had a

plan: They would arrange a joint presentation of the two theories. They asked for a copy of his 1842 "Sketch" to make it clear that Darwin had discovered evolution years earlier. Darwin was not cheered. He finally agreed to the plan, although he wrote to Hooker: "I dare say all is too late…. I hardly care about it. Do not waste much time. It is miserable in me to care at all about [who was first]." He was also troubled that they could not wait the several months needed to seek Wallace's approval for a joint reading. He could only hope that Wallace would not be annoyed.

Simultaneous Discoveries

Some writers have suggested that Darwin's theory soon gained wide acceptance because "evolution was in the air." Wallace's simultaneous discovery is often offered as evidence. Is it possible that, once the groundwork is laid, certain scientific advancements are inevitable? It's a complex question, but history does have many other cases of simultaneous discoveries. One of the most famous involves the telephone. In 1876, Scottish-American inventor Alexander Graham Bell applied for a patent for his "speaking telegraph." Hours later, American Elisha Gray requested a patent for a remarkably similar device. And earlier, in the 1670s, Englishman Isaac Newton and German Gottfried Leibniz independently developed the mathematics of calculus.

Darwin knew of Wallace and they had exchanged a few letters. Each knew the other was studying the nature of species, but Darwin never dreamed that they were on parallel paths. They were both honorable men, however, and neither was interested in undermining the other. The joint

presentation seemed to be a good compromise.

What was called the "joint paper" was presented to the Linnean Society, one of England's leading scientific organizations, on July 1, 1858, by Sir Charles Lyell and Sir Joseph Hooker. Darwin did not attend, partly because he was grief stricken over the death of his youngest child. There were fewer than fifty people at the meeting that introduced the idea of evolution through natural selection to the public, and there was no sudden outcry. The small audience remained silent. Huxley suggested that the opposition was not ready to attack the theory until they put on their armor.

Darwin put aside the several hundred pages he had

already written on his planned book, *Natural Selection*, and prepared a shorter version. The new book, still a substantial 400 pages, was published in November 1859 with the title *On the Origin of Species by Means of Natural Selection.* The public was now eager to

Darwin's theory was first made public in this room at the Linnean Society; pages from his original manuscript are also shown.

see it. The entire first edition of 1,250 copies was sold within hours; a second edition of 3,000 copies also disappeared quickly, and more followed. Those numbers are small by today's standards, but for a scientific book in the 19th century they constituted a best seller. Since then, the *Origin* has never once been out of print.

ON

THE ORIGIN OF SPECIES

BY MEANS OF NATURAL SELECTION,

OR THE

PRESERVATION OF FAVOURED RACES IN THE STRUGGLE
FOR LIFE.

BY CHARLES DARWIN, M.A.,
FELLOW OF THE ROYAL, GEOLOGICAL, LINNÆAN, ETC., SOCIETIES;
AUTHOR OF ' JOURNAL OF RESEARCHES DURING H. M. S. BEAGLE'S VOYAGE
ROUND THE WORLD.'

LONDON:
JOHN MURRAY, ALBEMARLE STREET.
1859.

The right of Translation is reserved.

Although the *Origin* was produced in just thirteen months of determined work, it was remarkably well argued. Darwin drew on his packed notebooks to provide page after page of examples

Despite Wallace, Darwin took intense delight in publishing the theory that had so long occupied his thoughts.

from more than 20 years of experience in collecting, sorting, experimenting, and analyzing. He led the reader step-by-step through the stages of natural selection, using the struggle for survival to show how a species could change over many generations in ways that enabled it to meet the challenges of its environment.

Darwin wrote with power and with clarity. He also wrote about the awe-inspiring beauty he saw in a constantly changing natural world, ending the book with these lines:

Alfred Russel Wallace
(1823–1913)

The early career of Alfred Russel Wallace was a combination of study and travel similar to Darwin's. In 1848, Wallace traveled to Africa and South America, a voyage about which he wrote a book. Unlike Darwin, Wallace was not from a wealthy family and he had to work hard to earn a living. He was in the Malay islands off the southeast coast of Asia from 1854 to 1862, and it was there that he came up with a theory of evolution so remarkably close to Darwin's.

"It is interesting to contemplate an entangled bank, clothed with many plants of many kinds, with birds singing in the bushes, with various insects flitting about, and with worms crawling through the damp earth, and to reflect that these elaborately constructed forms, so different from each other, and dependent on each other in so complex a manner, have all been produced by laws acting around us…. There is grandeur in this view of life, with its several powers, having been originally breathed into a few forms or into one; and that, whilst this planet has gone cycling on according to the fixed laws of gravity, from so simple a beginning endless forms most beautiful and wonderful have been, and are being, evolved."

For many readers, the most impressive thing about Darwin's book was the great simplicity of his argument. This simplicity led Huxley to declare, "how extremely

stupid" it was not to have thought of it himself. Darwin was understandably gratified. In a note to his publisher, he said, "I am infinitely pleased & proud at the appearance of my child." Wallace, still in Indonesia, was most impressed by the *Origin*. The evidence that Darwin had discovered natural selection first was overwhelming, and that made acceptance easier for Wallace. He also acknowledged that Darwin supported the theory with far more evidence than he, or any other scientist, could have managed.

More than a year had elapsed between the joint Darwin-Wallace paper in July 1858 and the publication of the *Origin* in November 1859. Response to the joint paper had been so muted that Darwin began to hope that the book might not create the storm of controversy he had feared. Huxley warned him that it would come, but that Darwin's friends would be ready for it. He referred to future critics as "the curs which will bark and yelp," but he told Darwin to keep in mind that "some of your friends…are endowed with a certain amount of combativeness…. I am sharpening up my claws & beak in readiness."

Clemence Royer (1830–1902) was the first to translate the *Origin* into French.

The storm came in early 1860, a few weeks after the book's publication, with a burst of angry reviews in journals and

newspapers, sermons by offended ministers, and letters to newspapers and to Darwin himself. Most of the criticism involved outrage over what was seen as an attack on the very foundation of religion. While Hooker, Huxley, and others were vigorous in their defense of the *Origin* and its author, the reactions of a few of Darwin's old friends and mentors were most disappointing. Adam Sedgwick told him in a long letter, "I have read your book with more pain than pleasure. Parts of it I admired greatly…other parts I read with absolute sorrow, because I think them utterly false and grievously mischievous."

John Henslow, too, as a minister, could not accept the idea of transmutation without the hand of God. Darwin could accept that from Henslow, but he had expected more from Lyell, who had urged him to publish and even helped present his paper! The geologist continued to support Darwin's work privately and to offer ideas for later editions, but he would not defend his friend publicly—he did not want to be part of a controversy that so threatened the established order.

Darwin was clearly troubled by the attacks that accused him of undermining Judeo-Christian beliefs. He is sometimes pictured as staying out of the fray by remaining isolated at Down House or at health resorts. In fact, far from avoiding the debate, he seems to have acted more as a behind-the-scenes strategist, often dashing off letters to his supporters, suggesting ways to counter some critical review or argumentative letter.

When he prepared the *Origin*'s second edition, immediately after the first, Darwin made an interesting choice: He changed the book's last sentence to show that there was room for God in the process of evolution, altering it to read: "There is grandeur in this view of life... having been originally breathed *by the Creator* into a few forms or into one." Still, this was not enough to quiet critics, who saw no room for God in Darwin's scheme of seemingly mechanical laws producing changes in plant and animal species.

The most dramatic confrontation between attackers and defenders of evolution took place at the Oxford University Museum of Natural History in June 1860.

The 1858 completion of the Oxford University Museum of Natural History showed the field's growing status as a science.

> ## "I should like to ask Professor Huxley…. Is it on his grandfather's or grandmother's side that the ape ancestry comes in?"
>
> –Bishop Samuel Wilberforce,
> in an attack on Darwin's theory

No member of the clergy was more outraged by the *Origin* than Samuel Wilberforce, the bishop of Oxford. He had already used his usual combination of wit and shrewd debating tactics to attack the book in a journal review. He was eager for this public chance to blast Darwin's theory out of the water once and for all. Bishop Wilberforce was aided by Richard Owen, the very scientist who had helped analyze Darwin's *Beagle* fossils. Owen seems to have been jealous of both Darwin and Huxley, so he willingly helped Bishop Wilberforce attack the *Origin*.

The Oxford meeting was packed with more than 700 people who listened with rapt attention to the bishop's clever performance. An eyewitness, the Reverend W.H. Freemantle, wrote: "The Bishop of Oxford attacked Darwin, at first playfully but at last in grim earnest." Then, turning to Huxley, he asked where all the evidence was, and said in his best bantering tone: "I should like to ask Professor Huxley, who is sitting by me, and is about to tear me to pieces when I have sat down, as to his belief in being descended from an ape. Is it on his grandfather's or his grandmother's side that

the ape ancestry comes in?" As the laughter died down, he concluded by saying that Darwin's writings were "contrary to the revelations of God in the Scriptures."

Huxley had wanted to avoid an argument, but he rose to the occasion. After showing how little Wilberforce understood of the science, Huxley said he felt no shame in sharing a common ancestor with an ape, but "I [would] be ashamed of a man, a man of restless and versatile intellect, who, not content with…success in his own sphere of activity, plunges into scientific questions with which he has no real acquaintance, only to obscure them by an aimless rhetoric, and distract the attention of the hearers from the real point at issue by eloquent digression, and skilled appeals to religious prejudice."

Huxley's powerful statement echoed throughout England for many months. It was seen by many as more than a defense of Darwin— it was science finally declaring independence from religion.

This cartoon shows Bishop Wilberforce and "Darwin's bulldog," Thomas Huxley.

12

The Great Man of Science

The controversy over publication of Darwin's *On the Origin of Species* raged over the next decade, but the debates became less heated soon after the Oxford meeting of 1860. Most of the opposition came from the clergy, who continued to see evolution as blasphemy, an attack on the Bible's account of creation. Still, a minority of ministers did support what was being called "Darwinism," saying they saw no conflict between this new theory and the Bible. Meanwhile, the majority of scientists not only accepted evolution, but saw it as a startling and exciting new way to look at life and the process of change.

Darwin benefited from people's growing acceptance of new ideas. Wonderful new inventions and scientific discoveries were becoming almost daily occurrences as the pace of change picked up speed over the last forty years of the century. Electric lights, telephones, cameras, phonographs, elevators, motion pictures, automobiles—all made their appearance between 1870

Elizabeth Blackwell wanted to be a doctor in order to help other women with health problems specific to females.

and 1900. In medical science, the Frenchman Louis Pasteur proved that tiny organisms called germs caused disease. At the same time, Scottish physician Joseph Lister showed that infections after surgeries could be reduced by 90 percent or more simply by using antiseptics. (In the past, surgeons thought nothing of reusing surgical needles and threads, which they kept in the buttonholes of their coats for easy access.) The work of Pasteur and Lister led to remarkable improvements in

Pasteur also created a heating process, known as "pasteurization," that kept harmful organisms from growing in food.

health care and ushered in the modern age of medicine.

The great innovations of these years created new public confidence in the work of physicians and scientists. Earlier in the century, science had been a part-time pursuit, practiced by men with other sources of income, such as positions in the ministry or family wealth. By the 1870s and 1880s, it was a field for full-time professionals, including a few women. In 1847, for example, American Maria Mitchell established the orbit of a new comet and became a leading astronomer; and two years later, English-born Elizabeth Blackwell became the first woman in America to receive a medical degree.

In this changing atmosphere people began to see Darwin in a new way. Instead of some wild revolutionary intent on

undermining Christianity, he was now viewed as something of a national treasure, England's great man of science. People began making pilgrimages to the village of Downe, hoping for a glimpse of the famous scientist.

In the early 1850s, Darwin still looked like a vigorous man entering middle age.

As the *Origin* was published in other countries after 1860, Darwin's fame spread. One country after another presented him with awards and degrees, and Cambridge University made him an honorary doctor of letters.

Although he shunned publicity, Darwin was pleased to have his contributions to science acknowledged. He had always had a good deal of personal ambition and confessed in his *Autobiography* that, from early in his career, "I was…ambitious to take a fair place among scientific men."

The success of the *Origin* encouraged him to begin work on three more books to complete his study of evolution. But in 1863, his work pace, as well as his enjoyment of his new prestige, was compromised by the most severe breakdown in health he had ever suffered. The old

Only 14 years later, not yet 60, Darwin looked surprisingly elderly and feeble.

symptoms, never absent for long, now became more severe. As before, these included trembling, vomiting, skin rashes, and exhaustion. Nothing the doctors tried seemed to help.

Cartoonists had great fun with the notion that humans were descended from apes—a distortion of Darwin's theory.

For the next four years, Darwin was an invalid, rarely able to work for more than an hour or two a day. Emma and the the house staff tended to him with great care, and he never lost his cheerfulness, even during his worst bouts of stomach cramps. He stopped shaving and let his beard grow. When the beard soon turned white, it only added to the general impression that Darwin, in a very short time, had become a frail old man. His health finally began to improve in late 1867. When he finally managed a trip to London later that year, even his friends did not recognize him.

In spite of his health miseries, Darwin continued to work every day. His mind was as sharp as ever and his curiosity just as lively. From 1860 on, he produced ten more books. The third of these books dealt with the idea that humans, too, had evolved from lower animals. He almost didn't tackle it, as he knew this was an explosive topic—as evidenced in the 1860 debate at Oxford. In a letter to Wallace, he had written that the evolution of humans was "the highest and

most interesting problem for the naturalist [but] I think I shall avoid the whole subject [because it's] so surrounded with prejudices."

Darwin finally decided to deal with the subject because he hoped to correct some of the misunderstandings generated by the *Origin*. He had tried to explain in the *Origin* that, in the distant past, humans and the great apes had both descended from simpler forms. His critics, including several cartoonists, twisted that statement, insisiting, "Mr. Darwin states that humans are descended from apes." Upon hearing this, a minister's wife is said to have exclaimed: "Heavens! If it is true, let us pray it doesn't become generally known."

In *The Descent of Man, and Selection in Relation to Sex*, published in 1871, Darwin explained how certain ancient animals had slowly evolved into several branches of higher life-forms, with the great apes in one branch and humans in another. People's interest in the subject soared when an explorer returned from central Africa with the first gorilla skin ever seen in Europe. But the clear evidence that Darwin supplied, such as the similar skeletal structures of humans and apes, did not stop the public mockery.

The Darwin Children

1. William Erasmus 1839–1914
2. Anne Elizabeth 1841–1851
3. Mary Eleanor 1842 (d. an infant)
4. Henrietta Emma 1843–1929
5. George Howard 1845–1912
6. Elizabeth 1847–1926
7. Francis 1848–1925
8. Leonard 1850–1943
9. Horace 1851–1928
10. Charles Waring 1856–1858

This male peacock's elegant display for the nearby female shows Darwin's theory of sexual selection in action.

The second half of the book developed his theory of sexual selection. Darwin pointed out that, in some species, males battled other males for the right to mate with females, while in other species, females selected males on the basis of strength, beauty, or other qualities. At a time when women were regarded as passive creatures, most scientists scorned this idea of female sexual selection. Nevertheless, the concept eventually became accepted—and is often used to explain the development of traits that appear to give an animal little advantage, such as the bright and cumbersome tail of the male peacock. Still, scientists continue to debate the details. As recently as May 2006, an issue of *American Naturalist* reported a study that showed females sometimes select *less* strong or handsome males, perhaps to

In *Expression*, Darwin made creative use of photographic images. These are from the section on expressions of joy.

give their species greater diversity.

The third and final sequel to the *On the Origin of Species* was titled *The Expression of the Emotions in Man and Animals*, published in 1872, in which Darwin showed that humans are not unique in using sounds, motions, and facial movements to express such emotions as love, hate, fear, and anxiety. Darwin had been filling notebooks with information on this topic ever since his and Emma's first child was born in 1839. He observed all of his children carefully, noting their facial expressions, movements, and sounds, and matching these with different emotions. The children didn't mind being observed, of course, especially when it involved trips to London's Regent's Park Zoo, which had acquired an orangutan named Jenny. Darwin was fascinated to see how similar Jenny's mannerisms and expressions were to those of his children. He added lots of photographs of humans and animals to the book, an unusual feature for a late-19th-century work. The illustrations helped make *The Expression of Emotions* a best seller.

Darwin had always had a tendency to become obsessed

with the subject at hand, whether it was coral reefs, barnacles, or evolution. Over the last 20 years of his life, his great passion was botany—the study of plants. Even as he was finishing his evolution series, he was already experimenting with, and writing about, plants. His detailed studies explored important new areas of botanical knowledge. He demonstrated, for example, the complicated characteristics that flowers develop to increase their chances of survival, including their method of arranging pollen for removal by insects.

Darwin's botanical work demonstrated two of his special traits: his great admiration for the beauties of nature, and his absolute delight in detailed and careful observation. The fields around Downe held several varieties of wild orchids, and he began studying them intently, when he really should have been writing the last of his evolution studies. He confessed that he often felt "quite guilty [but] there is to me incomparably more interest in observing than in writing." And, long after completing his book on orchids, he wrote in a letter to Hooker: "They are wonderful creatures, these Orchids, and I sometimes think with a glow of pleasure when

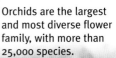

Orchids are the largest and most diverse flower family, with more than 25,000 species.

I remember making out some little point in their method of fertilisation."

As was true of Darwin throughout his life, his immense curiosity often led him in new directions. While on a seaside vacation with his family, for instance, he watched a common plant called a sundew as its leaf closed around a fly caught on the sticky surface. He dug up the sundew, replanted it at Down House, and conducted experiments. That led to an exhaustive study of carnivorous plants published in 1875. These plants, such as the familiar Venus flytrap, can chemically "digest" insects—which is why they're popularly known as "flesh-eating" plants!

Darwin's last book, published in 1881, just six months before his death, was one of his most popular, in spite of its rather unexciting title: *The Formation of Vegetable Mould Through the Action of Worms*. Darwin demonstrated that the earth's precious layer of life-supporting topsoil was created over thousands of years by the work of billions of worms digesting leaves and other organic materials. The popularity of this pioneering work was probably, at least in part, a reflection of the English people's great love of gardening.

This damselfly will soon be engulfed by this hungry Venus flytrap.

Publications by Charles Darwin

Journal of Researches into Geology and Natural History, 1839
Zoology of the Voyage of HMS Beagle, 1839–43
The Structure and Distribution of Coral Reefs, 1842
Geological Observations of Volcanic Islands, 1844
Geological Observations on South America, 1846
Four volumes on various families of barnacles, 1851–54
On the Origin of Species by Means of Natural Selection, 1859
Volume on orchid fertilization, 1859
Variation of Plants and Animals Under Domestication, 1868
The Descent of Man, and Selection in Relation to Sex, 1871
The Expression of Emotions in Man and Animals, 1872
Movement and Habits of Climbing Plants, 1875
Insectivorous Plants, 1875
The Effects of Cross and Self-Fertilisation in the Vegetable Kingdom, 1876
The Different Forms of Flowers on Plants of the Same Species, 1877
The Power of Movement in Plants, with Francis Darwin, 1880
The Formation of Vegetable Mould Through the Action of Worms, 1881
Autobiography of Charles Darwin, edited by Francis Darwin, 1887

From about 1870 on, as Darwin finished his evolution series and became more deeply involved in botany, his health steadily improved. His familiar symptoms did not disappear, but they became less frequent and less severe. While not robust, he could once again get around and managed short vacation trips with Emma to health spas on the seashore. Why the collapse followed by improvement? Most analysts believe that completion of the evolution series removed the great stress that had so much to do with Darwin's health miseries. In any case, he enjoyed better health over the last 10 or 12 years of his life than at any time since his days at Cambridge.

chapter 13

The Widening Influence

In the last years of his life, Charles Darwin continued to enjoy his position as the honored elder statesman of science. He was a member of more than 50 foreign scientific societies and wrote hundreds of letters—15,000 have been collected, so far! He was also active in Downe's village affairs, serving as justice of the peace and even attending church social functions.

Darwin continued to work until the very end of his life. Although his health was good, he worried about becoming so ill that he could not continue working. "When I am obliged to give up observation and experiment, I shall die," he said. A few weeks later, after a sudden series of heart attacks, he passed away quietly at Down

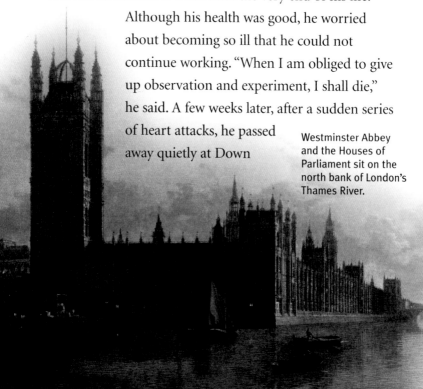

Westminster Abbey and the Houses of Parliament sit on the north bank of London's Thames River.

House on April 19, 1882. He was 73 years old. His last words: "Tell all my children to remember how good they have always been to me. I am not the least afraid of death."

The family had planned to have Darwin buried near his home, but his friends and supporters had other ideas. A special law was rushed through Parliament, setting up a state funeral with burial in Westminster Abbey. Huxley, Hooker, and Wallace were among the those who carried the coffin. Darwin then joined many of the great figures of England's history as he was interred in the great church near Sir Isaac Newton, another major figure in English science.

One of his few regrets had been that he had allowed his life to become too narrowly focused on scientific inquiry. "My mind," he wrote in his *Autobiography*, "seems to have become a kind of machine for grinding general laws out of large collections of facts…. If I had to live my life again I would have made a rule to read some poetry and listen to some music at least once every week."

Darwin's influence continued to grow long after his death, and his writings still provide a starting point for new areas of investigation in the 21st century. Over the years, his ideas have also contributed to the birth of entirely new branches of science, such as genetics and cellular biology.

One of the problems Darwin wrestled with involved the mechanics of heredity. How exactly were traits transmitted from parent to offspring? It was a puzzle that all breeders of plants and animals wondered about. Darwin tried to provide

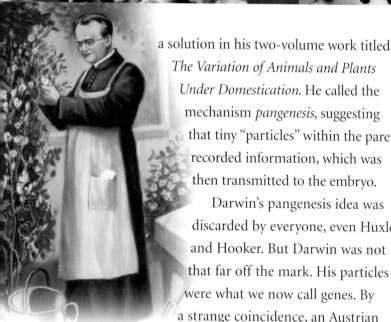

a solution in his two-volume work titled *The Variation of Animals and Plants Under Domestication*. He called the mechanism *pangenesis,* suggesting that tiny "particles" within the parent recorded information, which was then transmitted to the embryo.

Darwin's pangenesis idea was discarded by everyone, even Huxley and Hooker. But Darwin was not that far off the mark. His particles were what we now call genes. By a strange coincidence, an Austrian monk named Gregor Mendel was discovering genes during this same time period. For more than 10 years,

Mendel, now known as "the father of genetics," grew and tested 28,000 pea plants between 1856 and 1863.

Mendel experimented with pea plants. He discovered that some traits—such as tallness—were "dominant," and others— such as shortness—were "recessive." These traits were passed on to offspring according to predictable rules. Mendel published his results in 1866 in an obscure Austrian journal. There is no evidence that Darwin knew of this work, or that Mendel knew of Darwin.

Mendel's work was forgotten until around 1900, when three separate researchers, working on the problem of heredity, came across the journal article. Following Darwin and Mendel, they found that heredity works through special

cells that carry the particles of heredity, or genes.

In 1953, scientists Francis Crick and James Watson made the next great discovery in heredity. They found that genes consist of molecules of deoxyribose nucleic acid, or DNA. Then, in 2003, nearly 150 years after Darwin and Mendel, a team of scientists finished mapping the sequence of the three-billion chemical pairs that make up human DNA.

Quite apart from science, Darwin's theory of evolution through natural selection became part of people's thinking. For example, scholars found that businesses and companies evolved over time, and so did entire societies. Even the rise and fall of empires seemed to reveal the laws of evolution at work, as did the development of democracy in Great Britain and the United States.

The most striking application of Darwin's ideas to society was the brainchild of English philosopher Herbert Spencer. Spencer was an enthusiastic

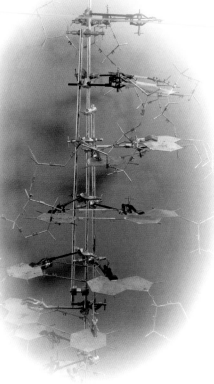

In their model, Crick and Watson used metal plates to show the coiled "double helix" structure of the DNA molecule.

advocate of the theory of evolution, and he invented a new term—"survival of the fittest"—as a substitute for "natural selection." The term became so popular that Darwin incorporated it into the later editions of the *Origin*, and people soon thought of it as Darwin's term.

In an essay published seven years before the *Origin*, Spencer had presented the idea that species evolved.

Spencer's most radical step was to apply the concept of survival of the fittest to societies. He argued that those people, or groups, who were best equipped for the struggle to survive would eventually rise to the top. Those less fit would sink to the bottom or die out. Many business leaders in Europe and America were thrilled with Spencer's theory, which became known as social Darwinism. The theory enabled them to believe that they were meant to succeed and amass huge fortunes because of their imagined superior intelligence, while their less-fit workers were destined to survive on starvation wages. The concept of social Darwinism helped persuade some government leaders that programs to help immigrants, the poor, or the disabled would interfere with the laws of nature.

Nonscientific applications of Darwin's ideas continued throughout the 20th century. Social Darwinism reached absurd extremes with the emergence of Fascism and Nazism in the 1920s. Both political philosophies were based on the notion of a "master race"—a superior racial or ethnic group that would triumph over all "inferior races." This was the theoretical basis for Adolf Hitler's monstrous attempt to exterminate certain groups during the Holocaust, which resulted in the slaughter of millions during World War II.

A very different reaction to Darwin's theory emerged among conservative Christian groups in the United States in the early 20th century. These groups, known as fundamentalists, insisted that Darwin's ideas were blasphemy; they wanted to present a literal interpretation of the Bible as scientific fact. This new antievolution appealed strongly

Jews, homosexuals, gypsies, and disabled people were the victims of Hitler's extreme distortion of the theory of evolution.

to many rural Americans, who felt that their values and way of life were being overwhelmed by an age of industrialization and rapid change.

Fundamentalist preachers toured the country, crying out against evolution—which was often distorted into the idea that humans had evolved from apes. Many rural states passed laws making it a crime to teach evolution. The matter reached a climax in 1925 when Tennessee teacher John T. Scopes was arrested and tried for teaching evolution in his science class.

The "Monkey Trial," as it became known, was conducted in a carnival atmosphere, surrounded by huge crowds, souvenir stands, country preachers, reporters, news photographers, and even a monkey dressed in human clothes. As expected, Scopes was found guilty of teaching evolution and was fined $100, though the court refused to consider whether the Tennessee

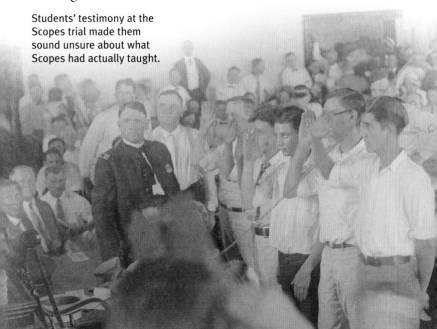

Students' testimony at the Scopes trial made them sound unsure about what Scopes had actually taught.

law was constitutional. Finally, in 1968, the Supreme Court declared all state antievolution laws unconstitutional.

The division between those who accept evolution and those who believe in a literal interpretation of the Bible has continued into the 21st century. In an effort to influence schools, fundamentalists in the 1960s began advocating "creation science." Nonetheless, courts have consistently ruled that the Bible's creation story is religion, not science, and cannot be taught as such. But fundamentalists continue to be concerned that their children are being taught a subject that undermines their family's religious beliefs.

Intelligent Design

According to intelligent design (or ID), beings as complex as humans can only be understood as the creation of an intelligent designer, such as God. Starting in the 1990s, some claimed ID should be taught alongside evolution, or as an alternative. In 2005, a Pennsylvania school board insisted that biology teachers discuss ID, but a judge later struck down the policy, calling the idea "a mere re-labeling of creationism, and not a scientific theory."

What would Darwin say about the continuing debate? "As for myself," he wrote, "I believe I have acted rightly in steadily following and devoting my life to Science. I feel no remorse from having committed any great sin." His only real regret was "that I have not done more direct good to my fellow creatures."

chapter **14**

Darwin's Legacy Today

M eet the "fishapod." This unusual creature lived about 375 million years ago. When its fossil remains were chipped from rocks in northern Canada and reported in the April 2006 issue of *Nature,* world attention was once again focused on Charles Darwin. In fact, he and his theories have never been out of the news for long since *On the Origin of Species* was first published in 1859.

The fishapod, which probably grew to a length of more than nine feet, was given the scientific name *Tiktaalik* (from an Inuit word meaning "large fish in stream"). Scientists have determined that this creature lived at a key time in evolutionary history—the point at which some species of fish were evolving into four-legged creatures that could spend at least part of their time on land. In other words, the fishapod is

When dissected, the fishapod's fins showed the beginnings of hands, complete with five fingerlike bones.

This car plaque alters the popular Christian fish symbol into the image of a transitional form.

a link between life in the sea and life on land. Scientists call such creatures "transitional forms," but most people prefer to call them "missing links."

Why are missing links so important? The answer is that they are evidence—or proof—that Darwin was right in saying that more advanced species gradually evolved from earlier, more primitive species. One of the strongest criticisms of the *Origin* was that Darwin offered no evidence of transitional forms. Where, the critics wanted to know, were the fossils that would prove Darwin's claim? He could only insist that the links were there and that they would be discovered over time.

The fishapod provided one of the transitional forms Darwin had promised, and scientists were keenly aware of its importance. One of the discoverers told other team members: "This is not some archaic branch of the animal kingdom. This is our branch. You're looking at your great-great-great-great cousin!"

Dozens of other transitional forms have been added to the fossil record in the 150 years since the

The Fossil Record

Gathering fossil evidence of transitional forms has proven difficult for several reasons. For one thing, fossils form under very special circumstances. Most remains of plants and animals decay, or are consumed, before the material in which they are embedded hardens. Even then, it's hard to find them—scientists estimate that 99.9 percent of the fossil record has not been discovered!

Origin was published. By coincidence, one of these forms was discovered in 1861, just as Darwin's critics were asking where they were. The discovery, named *Archaeopteryx*, looked like a small dinosaur, but had feathers and could fly. Scientists had known for some time that dinosaurs and birds were related. Here was a transitional form establishing the fact.

All sorts of other transitional forms have been found, including links in the evolution of horses and reptiles. The missing links between primates and humans have also slowly been unearthed. Well into the 20th century, these forms helped show that eastern Africa was likely home to the first humans.

Until Darwin, people felt the world was stable. All life-forms had been created at one time and they had not changed since—although some creatures, like dinosaurs, had become extinct. Darwin wrenched people's thinking out of that comfortable sameness. In fact, one reason some people were so furious about Darwinism was that it demanded an entirely new worldview—one based on change, rather than stability. As the great philosopher Bertrand Russell put it, "Darwin threw down a challenge to the old rigidities, and his doctrine of evolution made everything a matter of degree, obliterating the absoluteness of white-and-black, right-and-wrong.… And in the mush of compromise all the old splendid certainties dissolved."

Darwin's theories, and his countless examples of evolutionary change, continue to influence thinking in many fields, far beyond plants and animals. Psychologists, for

example, study human (and animal) behavior in terms of how emotions and ways of thinking evolve over time. Astronomers see evolution in the formation of galaxies and in the life and death of stars. Even linguistics, the study of languages, deals with the way languages evolve—for example, the addition of new verbs like "to google" to common speech and dictionaries.

Darwin used his incredible storehouse of evidence to revise and modify his own conclusions. One aspect of his great genius was his ability to gather evidence for a remarkably long time, as well as his incredible ability to generalize. "From my early youth," he wrote in his *Autobiography*, "I have had the strongest desire to understand whatever I observed—that is, to group all facts under some general laws. These causes combined have given me the patience to reflect or ponder for any number of years over any unexplained problem."

The 10-pound Note

In 2001, England celebrated Darwin's relevance to the 21st century by printing his picture on the 10-pound note (roughly equivalent to 18 U.S. or 21 Canadian dollars). Darwin's image replaced the picture of Charles Dickens, the towering literary figure of the 19th century. People have speculated about the reasons for the change. Some have joked that Darwin had the better beard. But most feel that the switch simply showed Darwin's greater significance to today's world.

No other individual in modern times has so radically changed how we think. Other great thinkers have developed powerful ideas that shook the world—but only for a time. Karl Marx's ideas led to the 20th century's experiments with Communism, for example, most notably in the Soviet Union, but most of those experiments had failed by the end of the century. Similarly, the writings of Sigmund Freud provided the starting point for early exploration in psychiatry, but Freud's concepts, too, have been overshadowed by newer theories.

By contrast, Darwin's ideas have been consistently validated. Even as we approach the bicentennial of his birth, he remains as relevant to the 21st century as he was to the 19th. In fact, one of the most exciting things about Darwin is how his extraordinary genius continues to shed light on contemporary events. Day after day we use the incredibly detailed lense he provided: Is the earth getting warmer? Can we end the scourge of AIDS? Can hydrogen fuel replace oil? Issues like these involve thinking in terms of evolutionary change.

Today Darwin's theories are hailed by scientists. James Watson, the famous DNA scientist, says, "Let us not beat around the bush—the common assumption that evolution through natural selection is a 'theory'…is wrong. Evolution is…as well substantiated as any other natural law, whether the Law of Gravity [or] the Laws of Motion." Paleontologist Niles Eldredge is even more direct: "We evolved. No doubt about it. Darwin was right."

If Darwin were alive today, he would likely be proud of his legacy, but humble as well. He summed up his lifelong search for truth with these words: "Whenever I have found out that I have blundered, or that my work has been imperfect…it has been my greatest comfort to say hundreds of times to myself that 'I have worked as hard and as well as I could, and no man can do more than this.'"

From early hominid to modern human, Darwin paved the way for a scientific understanding of our origins.

Events in the Life of Charles Darwin

August 1831
Darwin receives invitation to sail on HMS *Beagle* as the ship's naturalist.

1828–1831
Darwin finishes his ministry education at Cambridge University.

February 12, 1809
Charles Darwin is born in Shrewsbury, England.

August–September 1834
Beagle visits the Galapagos Islands. Darwin begins to wonder about evolution.

1838
Darwin first develops theory of natural selection.

1825–1827
Darwin studies medicine at Edinburgh University.

October 1836
Beagle returns to England after a voyage of almost five years.

1837
Darwin starts first notebook on evolution, working secretly.

1837–1842
Publication of books based on *Beagle* voyage spreads Darwin's fame.

1839
Darwin marries Emma Wedgwood. First of their 10 children is born.

December 1831
HMS *Beagle* sets sail.

1842
Darwins move to Down House, outside London.

1868–1872
Darwin publishes three more books on evolution, completing the series.

April 19, 1882
Charles Darwin dies at Down House. He is later buried in Westminster Abbey.

July 1860
Evolution is debated at Oxford meeting of the Royal Academy.

June 1858
Alfred Russel Wallace sends Darwin his essay on evolution. Friends arrange a joint presentation of the theory.

1842–1846
Darwin completes three volumes on geology and two private summaries of his theory of evolution.

November 1859
On the Origin of Species is published.

1867–1881
As his health improves, Darwin completes several books on orchids and other plants.

1863–1867
Poor health limits Darwin's work.

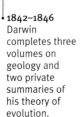

1846–1854
Still reluctant to publish his theory of evolution, Darwin spends eight years studying barnacles.

Today
Darwin's legacy continues.

Bibliography

Appleman, Philip, ed. *Charles Darwin. The Origin of Species*. NY: W.W. Norton & Co.,1975; 1979.

Barlow, Nora, ed. *Autobiography of Charles Darwin 1809-1882*. NY: W.W. Norton & Co., 1958; 2005.

Browne, Janet. *Charles Darwin. Voyaging. A Biography*. New York: Alfred A. Knopf, 1995.

_____.*Charles Darwin. The Power of Place*. Vol. II of *A Biography*. NY: Alfred A. Knopf, 2002.

Bryson, Bill. *A Short History of Nearly Everything*. NY: Broadway Books, 2003.

Darwin, Francis, ed. *Charles Darwin. Selected Letters on Evolution and Origin of Species with an Autobiographical Chapter*. NY: Dover Publications, Inc., 1958; 2004. [Reprint of 1892 edition]

Eldredge, Niles. *Darwin: Discovering the Tree of Life*. NY: W.W. Norton & Company, 2005.

Gamlin, Linda. *Evolution*. NY: Dorling Kindersley Publishing,1993.

Jones, Steven, ed. *Charles Darwin.The Voyage of the Beagle*. NY: The Modern Library, 2001.

Keynes, Randal. *Darwin, His Daughter & Human Evolution*. NY: Riverhead Books, 2001.

Lawson, Kristan. *Darwin and Evolution*. Chicago: Chicago Review Press, Inc., 2003.

Moorehead, Alan. *Darwin and the Beagle*. NY: Penguin Books, 1971.

Porter, Duncan M. and Peter W. Graham, eds. *The Portable Darwin*. NY: Penguin Books, 1993.

Simpson, George Gaylord, ed. *The Book of Darwin*. NY: Washington Square Press,1982.

Stefoff, Rebecca. *Charles Darwin and the Evolution Revolution*. NY: Oxford University Press, 1996

Sullivan, Walter, ed. *Charles Darwin. The Voyage of the Beagle*. NY: New American Library, 1972.

Watson, James D. ed. *Darwin: The Indelible Stamp*. Philadelphia: Running Press, 2005.

Works Cited

p. 6 "wretched-looking little weeds…" *Darwin: The Indelible Stamp*, 252; p. 7 "that mystery of mysteries…" *Darwin: The Indelible Stamp*, 255; p. 9 "the atmosphere at the Mount…" *Evolution Revolution*, 19; p. 9 "her death-bed…" *Autobiography*, 12; p. 10 "Nothing could have been worse…" *Autobiography*, 26; p. 12 "Organic life beneath…" *Darwin & Evolution*, 15; p. 12 "I had a strong taste for angling…" *Autobiography*, 26; p. 12 "I do not believe…" *Autobiography*, 39; p. 13 "When I left the school…" *Selected Letters*, 9; p. 14 "I had strong and diversified tastes…" *The Book of Darwin*, 36; p. 14 "watching the habits of birds…" *The Book of Darwin*, 36; p. 14 "This was the best part…" *The Book of Darwin*, 36; p. 14 "the kindest man I ever knew…" *Autobiography*, 27; p. 14–15 "You care for nothing…" *Darwin: Discovering the Tree of Life*, 22; p. 15 "The two cases fairly haunted me…" *The Book of Darwin*, 37; p. 18 "a horrid smoky wilderness…" *Evolution Revolution*, 36; p. 20 "Upon the whole…" *Autobiography*, 58; p. 20 "We used often to dine together…" *Autobiography*, 52; p. 20 "I stick fast in the mud…" *Darwin and the Beagle*, 26; p. 22 "Alas, it ejected…" *Autobiography*, 53; p. 22 "No poet ever felt more delighted…" *The Book of Darwin*, 43; p. 23 "Nothing before had ever made me…" *Evolution Revolution*, 38; p. 24 "a burning zeal…" *Autobiography*, 57; p. 26 "The Voyage of the Beagle…" *The Book of Darwin*, 51; p. 26 "on so small a circumstance…" *The Book of Darwin*, 51; p. 27; "But if it had not…" *Evolution Revolution*, 42; p. 28 "If you can find…" *Evolution Revolution*, 42; p. 28 "the pursuit of Natural History…" *Selected Letters*, 124–125; p. 29 "you and Charles…" *Selected Letters*, 125; p. 29 "My dear Father…" *Autobiography*, 191; p. 30 "I would have to be…" *Darwin and the Beagle*, 33; p. 30 "very happy to have…" *Darwin and the Beagle*, 33; p. 33 "My Dear Susan…" *Selected Letters*, 127; p. 33 "he was ever one…" *Darwin and the Beagle*, 25; p. 34 "No vessel has been fitted…" *Darwin and the Beagle*, 38; p. 34 "a birthday for…" *Darwin and the Beagle*, 38; p. 35 "a glorious day…" *Evolution Revolution*, 37; p. 36–37 "The delight one experiences…" *Voyage of the Beagle*, 12; p. 37–38 "I can confidently express…" *Selected Letters*,

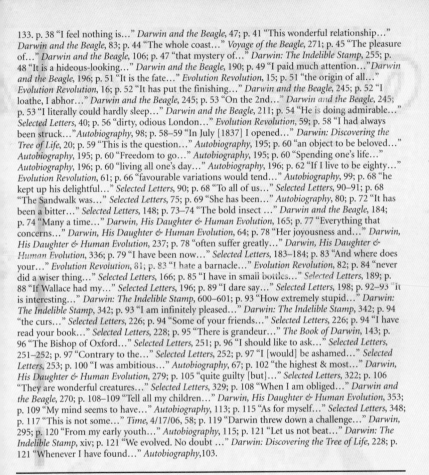

133. p. 38 "I feel nothing is…" *Darwin and the Beagle*, 47; p. 41 "This wonderful relationship…" *Darwin and the Beagle*, 83; p. 44 "The whole coast…" *Voyage of the Beagle*, 271; p. 45 "The pleasure of…" *Darwin and the Beagle*, 106; p. 47 "that mystery of…" *Darwin: The Indelible Stamp*, 255; p. 48 "It is a hideous-looking…" *Darwin and the Beagle*, 190; p. 49 "I paid much attention…"*Darwin and the Beagle*, 196; p. 51 "It is the fate…" *Evolution Revolution*, 15; p. 51 "the origin of all…" *Evolution Revolution*, 16; p. 52 "It has put the finishing…" *Darwin and the Beagle*, 245; p. 52 "I loathe, I abhor…" *Darwin and the Beagle*, 245; p. 53 "On the 2nd…" *Darwin and the Beagle*, 245; p. 53 "I literally could hardly sleep…" *Darwin and the Beagle*, 211; p. 54 "He is doing admirable…" *Selected Letters*, 40; p. 56 "dirty, odious London…" *Evolution Revolution*, 59; p. 58 "I had always been struck…"*Autobiography*, 98; p. 58–59 "In July [1837] I opened…" *Darwin: Discovering the Tree of Life*, 20; p. 59 "This is the question…" *Autobiography*, 195; p. 60 "an object to be beloved…" *Autobiography*, 195; p. 60 "Freedom to go…" *Autobiography*, 195; p. 60 "Spending one's life…" *Autobiography*, 196; p. 60 "living all one's day…" *Autobiography*, 196; p. 62 "If I live to be eighty…" *Evolution Revolution*, 61; p. 66 "favourable variations would tend…" *Autobiography*, 99; p. 68 "he kept up his delightful…" *Selected Letters*, 90; p. 68 "To all of us…" *Selected Letters*, 90–91; p. 68 "The Sandwalk was…" *Selected Letters*, 75; p. 69 "She has been…" *Autobiography*, 80; p. 72 "It has been a bitter…" *Selected Letters*, 148; p. 73–74 "The bold insect …" *Darwin and the Beagle*, 184; p. 74 "Many a time…" *Darwin, His Daughter & Human Evolution*, 165; p. 77 "Everything that concerns…" *Darwin, His Daughter & Human Evolution*, 64; p. 78 "Her joyousness and…" *Darwin, His Daughter & Human Evolution*, 237; p. 78 "often suffer greatly…" *Darwin, His Daughter & Human Evolution*, 336; p. 79 "I have been now…" *Selected Letters*, 183–184; p. 83 "And where does your…" *Evolution Revolution*, 81; p. 83 "I hate a barnacle…" *Evolution Revolution*, 82; p. 84 "never did a wiser thing…" *Selected Letters*, 166; p. 85 "I have in small bottles…" *Selected Letters*, 189; p. 88 "If Wallace had my…" *Selected Letters*, 196; p. 89 "I dare say…" *Selected Letters*, 198; p. 92–93 "It is interesting…" *Darwin: The Indelible Stamp*, 600–601; p. 93 "How extremely stupid…" *Darwin: The Indelible Stamp*, 342; p. 93 "I am infinitely pleased…" *Darwin: The Indelible Stamp*, 342; p. 94 "the curs…" *Selected Letters*, 226; p. 94 "Some of your friends…" *Selected Letters*, 226; p. 94 "I have read your book…" *Selected Letters*, 228; p. 95 "There is grandeur…" *The Book of Darwin*, 143; p. 96 "The Bishop of Oxford…" *Selected Letters*, 251; p. 96 "I should like to ask…" *Selected Letters*, 251–252; p. 97 "Contrary to the…" *Selected Letters*, 252; p. 97 "I [would] be ashamed…" *Selected Letters*, 253; p. 100 "I was ambitious…" *Autobiography*, 67; p. 102 "the highest & most…" *Darwin, His Daughter & Human Evolution*, 279; p. 105 "quite guilty [but]…" *Selected Letters*, 322; p. 106 "They are wonderful creatures…" *Selected Letters*, 329; p. 108 "When I am obliged…" *Darwin and the Beagle*, 270; p. 108–109 "Tell all my children…" *Darwin, His Daughter & Human Evolution*, 353; p. 109 "My mind seems to have…" *Autobiography*, 113; p. 115 "As for myself…" *Selected Letters*, 348; p. 117 "This is not some…" *Time*, 4/17/06, 58; p. 119 "Darwin threw down a challenge…" *Darwin*, 295; p. 120 "From my early youth…" *Autobiography*, 115; p. 121 "Let us not beat…" *Darwin: The Indelible Stamp*, xiv; p. 121 "We evolved. No doubt …" *Darwin: Discovering the Tree of Life*, 228; p. 121 "Whenever I have found…" *Autobiography*,103.

For Further Study

If you're ever in England, you can plan a visit to Down House; otherwise, just visit its Web site at: http://www.english-heritage.org.uk/server/show/ConProperty.102

Loads of information about Darwin, his life, and plans for an international day of celebration coinciding with the bicentennial of his birth and the 150th anniversary of the publication of the *Origin* in 2009 can be found at: http://www.darwinday.org

The University of California at Berkeley maintains an extensive educational site on evolution at: http://evolution.berkeley.edu/evolibrary/home.php

An incredible and extensive exhibit on Darwin is currently traveling to New York, Boston, Toronto, and London. For more information, visit: http://www.amnh.org/exhibitions/darwin/

Index

Archaeopteryx 118

Autobiography of Charles Darwin 58, 100, 107, 109, 119

Beagle, HMS
  description 31, 34, 35
  preparations, expedition 26–53
  map 52

Butler, Dr. Samuel 10, 14

Cambridge Univ. 18, 19, 24, 100

Chagas's disease 71–73

Chambers, Robert 74, 87

Darwin, Anne ["Annie"] (daughter) 67, 77–78, 102

Darwin, Caroline (sister) 9, 10

Darwin, Catherine (sister) 10, 45

Darwin, Charles
  education 10–11, 13, 14–17, 19–24
  family 8–10, 62, 67, 83, 85–86, 90, 102
  health 35, 69, 70–73, 100–101, 107
  legacy 109–121
  life
    childhood, adolescence 8–15
    early travels 18–19
    Beagle expedition 26–53
    marriage 59–61
    family life in England 62–69
    death and funeral 108–109
    physical appearance and character 31, 33, 38, 43, 53, 100
    religious beliefs 77, 79
  research on evolution. *See* evolution, theories of C. Darwin
  research on zoology 70, 82, 83–84
  scientific reputation 40, 54, 70, 75, 84, 100, 108
  timeline 122–123

Darwin, Dr. Erasmus (grandfather) 11–12, 45

Darwin, Dr. Robert (father) 8, 9, 12, 14, 17–19, 27–30

Darwin, Emma Wedgwood (wife) 18-19, 60–61, 67–69, 76–77, 101, 107

Darwin, Erasmus "Ras" (brother) 10, 13–14, 17, 18, 56

Darwin, Francis (son) 84, 102

Darwin, Marianne (sister) 9

Darwin, Susan (sister) 8, 33, 53

Darwin, Susannah Wedgwood (mother) 8, 9–10, 12

Darwin, William E. (son) 62, 102

The Descent of Man, and Selection in Relation to Sex 102–103, 107

Down House 66, 67–68, 69, 72, 76, 77

Earle, Augustus 36, 37

Edinburgh University 14, 16–17

"Essay" 74, 79, 81

evolution
  controversy. *See* religious aspects
  and linguistics 119
  natural selection 66, 67, 74, 90, 91, 111–112
  sexual selection 103
  and social sciences 112–113
  survival of the fittest 112
  taught in schools 114–115
  theories of C. Darwin
    development 63–67, 74, 75, 79–87
    going public 88–97
    inclusion of God 95
    observations during *Beagle* voyage 42, 44, 47, 50–51, 57–59
    publications 55, 62–63, 100, 101. *See also specific titles*
  theories of Erasmus Darwin 11–12, 75
  transition species 116–118

The Expression of Emotions in Man and Animals 104, 107

fishapod (*Tiktaalik*) 116–117

FitzRoy, Captain Robert
  character 30, 32, 38
  relationship with D. 38–39, 43

The Formation of Vegetable Mould Through the Action of Worms 106, 107

fossils 40-41, 44, 45, 54, 58, 116–118

Fox, William Darwin (cousin) 22, 83

Gould, John 55–57, 62

Great Exhibition, Crystal Palace 86, 87

Henslow, John Stevens
  as Darwin's teacher 20–21, 23, 24
  reaction to *Origin* 94
  support for Darwin 26, 30–31, 40, 54, 55, 62

Hooker, Sir Joseph
  as a friend 79, 109
  initial reaction to Darwin's theory 80–81
  presentation of theory 88–89, 90

  support for Darwin 84, 94

Humboldt, Baron Alexander von 24, 25

Huxley, Thomas H.
  career 84
  support for Darwin 84, 92–93, 94, 96–97
  views on those opposing D. 90

Indonesia 88, 92, 93

Industrial Revolution 56, 63

intelligent design 115

inventions 11, 12, 86–87, 89, 98–11

Lamarck, Jean-Baptiste 45

lifestyle of the privileged class 9, 13, 17, 21, 37, 76

London 55, 56, 62, 64, 104

Lyell, Sir Charles
  career 44, 45, 71
  as a friend 79, 94
  presentation of D. 's theory 88–89, 90
  support for Darwin 55, 70, 88–89

Maer 13, 26

Malthus, Thomas 64–65, 88

"Monkey Trial" 114–115

the Mount 8–9, 19, 25, 28, 30, 54

Natural Selection 86, 87, 90

On the Origin of the Species by Means of Natural Selection 90–97, 102, 107, 112

Owen, Richard 56, 57, 58, 62, 96

Oxford University Museum 95, 96

pottery, Wedgwood 12

religious aspects
  beliefs of Charles Darwin 77, 79
  beliefs of Emma Darwin 76–77
  Bible 41–42, 44, 45, 50, 59, 64, 77, 98, 113
  controversy over Darwin's theory 74–75, 80–81, 82, 93–97, 101–102, 113–115
  fundamentalism 113–115
  inclusion of God in *Origin* 95

Royer, Clemence 93

science. *See also* inventions
  astronomy 99, 119
  botany 77, 81, 85, 105–106
  creation 115
  fossil record 40–41, 44, 45, 54, 58, 116–118
  genetics 109–111

geology 23-25, 40, 44, 46, 62, 70, 71
medical 15, 98, 99
natural history 16–17, 25, 28
navigation 27
ornithology 49-50, 55-57, 64, 65, 85-86
patterns vs. details 23–24, 51, 119
professionals and funding 55, 99
psychology and emotions 104, 107, 118–119
public interest in the 1800s 21, 54, 85
simultaneous discoveries 89
zoology 21-23, 62, 70, 82-84, 102, 106

Sedgwick, Adam 23, 24, 25, 54, 94
Shrewsbury Gram. School 10-11, 13
"Sketch" 74, 89
social Darwinism 112–113
South America
    Argentina 39, 40, 41
    Brazil 36, 41, 52
    Chile 44–45
    Galapagos Islands 46–51
    gauchos 38, 39
    Tierra del Fuego 42–43
Spencer, Herbert 111–112
The Variation of Animals and Plants Under Domestication 107, 110

Vestiges of the Natural History of Creation 74–75, 87
Wallace, Alfred Russel 88–90, 92, 101, 109
Wedgwood, Josiah (g. father) 11, 12
Wedgwood, Josiah II (uncle) 13, 18, 26, 28–30, 61
Wedgwood family 11, 27–28
Westminster Abbey 108, 109
Wilberforce, Bishop Samuel 96–97
William IV, King of England 32, 33
World War II and the Holocaust 113
Zoology of the Voyage of HMS Beagle 70–71, 107

Acknowledgments

This book has evolved through the creative input of several people. My thanks to Beth Sutinis, DK Publishing Director, for making the project possible, to Alisha Niehaus, whose gentle, constructive editing kept it on track, to Professor Robert J. Richards of the University of Chicago for his expert assistance, and to my wife, Sharon, for the many creative hours of research and discussion.

Picture Credits

The photographs in this book are used with permission and through the courtesy of (t=top; b=bottom; c=center; l=left; r=right): DK Images: p. 1 Down House/Natural History Museum/Dave King; p.12 Judith Miller/Woolley and Wallis; p. 23 Down House/Natural History Museum; p. 25 Bartomiej Zaranek; p. 27 Judith Miller/Lyon & Turr Ltd.; p. 40 Dave King; pp. 105, 123btr Pawel Wojcik; p. 106 Kim Taylor & Jane Burton; p. 111 Dave King/ Science Museum, London.
New York Public Library: pp. 2–3, 5, 56, 57, 58, 60, 71, 92, 97, 100t & b, 101, 123tc. The Granger Collection: pp.7, 122bl. American Museum of Natural History: pp. 8, 9, 10, 14, 18, 35, 39, 41, 62, 65, 81, 122tl, 122br.
Bridgeman Art Library: p. 11 Darwin College; p. 15 Biblioteque de la Faculte de Medecine; p. 16 University of Edinburgh; p. 30 Royal Naval College; p. 36 Naional Library of Australia; p. 42 Down House; p. 76 Institut National de Recherche Pedagogique; p. 93 Archive Larousse. English Heritage Photo Library: p. 17; pp. 61 (Darwin's Heirloom Trust), 67, 77, 83, 122c, 123bl, Johathan Bailey; pp. 66, 69, 123tl Nigel Corrie.
Corbis: pp. 21, 32 Historical Picture Archive; p. 22 Cambridge University Library; p. 43, 85 Corbis; pp. 46, 122tc George D. Lepp; p. 47 Craig Lovell; p. 48 Hubert Stadler; pp. 48–49 Wolfgang Kaehler; p. 50l, Martin Harvey; pp. 54–55, 63 Stapleton Collection; p. 59 Archivo Iconografico, S.A.; pp. 64, 122tr Kevin Schafer; p. 84 Chris Hellier; p.103 Horst Ossinger; pp.108, 123tr Fine Art Photographic Library; p. 110, 114 Bettman; pp. 120–121 James W. Porter. Art Resource: p.38 HIP. Syndics of Cambridge University Library: pp. 28, 44–45, 78. Getty Images: pp. 50c & r, 51, 75, 88–87, 95, 98, 111, 113, 115; p. 70 National Geographic; pp. 90, 99 Time & Life Pictures. Dwight Kuhn: p. 72. Angelo Hornak Photo Library: p. 79. Library of Congress: p. 91, 112, 123bc. The Image Works: p. 104 NMPFT/SSPL. Vireo: p. 116 Ted Daeschler/Academy of Natural Sciences. Valiant Enterprises: p.117, 123blr. Bank of England: p.119.
BORDER PICTURES, left to right: Dorling Kindersley/Dave King/Down House/National History Museum; Getty Images/National Geographic; American Museum of Natural History; Dorling Kindersley/Dave King/ Down House/National History Museum; English Heritage Photo Library/Darwin Heirloom's Trust; Dorling Kindersley; Bridgeman Art Library/Down House; Dorling Kindersley/Down House/National History Museum; New York Public Library; New York Public Library; English Heritage Photo Library/Nigel Corrie; Library of Congress; New York Public Library.

127

About the Author

David C. King is the author of more than 70 books for children and young adults, including DK's popular *Children's Encyclopedia of American History*. His wife, Sharon, shares many research and writing projects, and they co-authored an award-winning book on the Statue of Liberty. Their home is in New England's beautiful Berkshire Mountains.

Other DK Biographies you'll enjoy:

Albert Einstein
by Frieda Wishinsky
ISBN 978-0-7566-1247-4 paperback
ISBN 978-0-7566-1248-1 hardcover

Helen Keller
by Leslie Garrett
ISBN 978-0-7566-0339-7 paperback
ISBN 978-0-7566-0488-2 hardcover

Gandhi
by Amy Pastan
ISBN 978-0-7566-2111-7 paperback
ISBN 978-0-7566-2112-4 hardcover

John F. Kennedy
by Howard S. Kaplan
ISBN 978-0-7566-0340-3 paperback
ISBN 978-0-7566-0489-9 hardcover

Martin Luther King, Jr.
by Amy Pastan
ISBN 978-0-7566-0342-7 paperback
ISBN 978-0-7566-0491-2 hardcover

Amelia Earhart
by Tanya Lee Stone
ISBN 978-0-7566-2552-8 paperback
ISBN 978-0-7566-2553-5 hardcover

Princess Diana
by Joanne Mattern
ISBN 978-0-7566-1614-4 paperback
ISBN 978-0-7566-1613-7 hardcover

Eleanor Roosevelt
by Kem Knapp Sawyer
ISBN 978-0-7566-1496-6 paperback
ISBN 978-0-7566-1495-9 hardcover

George Washington
by Lenny Hort
ISBN 978-0-7566-0835-4 paperback
ISBN 978-0-7566-0832-3 hardcover

Nelson Mandela
by Laaren Brown & Lenny Hort
ISBN 978-0-7566-2109-4 paperback
ISBN 978-0-7566-2110-0 hardcover

Harry Houdini
by Vicki Cobb
ISBN 978-0-7566-1245-0 paperback
ISBN 978-0-7566-1246-7 hardcover

Abraham Lincoln
by Tanya Lee Stone
ISBN 978-0-7566-0834-7 paperback
ISBN 978-0-7566-0833-0 hardcover

Look what the critics are saying about DK Biography!

"…highly readable, worthwhile overviews for young people…"—*Booklist*

"This new series from the inimitable DK Publishing brings together the usual brilliant photography with a historian's approach to biography subjects."
—*Ingram Library Services*

Charles
Darwin

David C. King

DK PUBLISHING

LONDON, NEW YORK, MUNICH,
MELBOURNE, and DELHI

Editor : Alisha Niehaus
Publishing Director : Beth Sutinis
Designer : Mark Johnson Davies
Senior Designer : Tai Blanche
Art Director : Dirk Kaufman
Photo Research : Anne Burns Images
Production : Ivor Parker
DTP Designer : Kathy Farias

First American Edition, 2007

07 08 09 10 11 10 9 8 7 6 5 4 3 2 1
Published in the United States
by DK Publishing
375 Hudson Street, New York,
New York 10014

DK books are available at special discounts
when purchased in bulk for sales
promotions, premiums, fund-raising,
or educational use. For details, contact:

DK Publishing Special Markets
375 Hudson Street
New York, New York 10014
SpecialSales@dk.com

A catalog record for this book is available
from the Library of Congress.

Printed and bound in China
by South China Printing Co., Ltd.

Photography credits:
Front cover: © English Heritage Photo
Library/Jeremy Richards
Back Cover: © Bridgeman Art Library/
Down House

Discover more at
www.dk.com

Contents

Prologue
A Most Unusual Voyage
6–7

Chapter 1
"A Very Ordinary Boy"
8–15

Chapter 2
The Search for Direction
16–25

Chapter 3
Signing On
26–33

Chapter 4
The Voyage of the Beagle Begins
34–45

Chapter 5
The Beagle in the Galapagos
46–51

Chapter 6
Home and a New Life
52–61

Chapter 7
The Countryman's Doubts
62–69

Chapter 8
Health Matters
70–73

Chapter 9
"Gleams of Light"
74–81

Chapter 10
**Delay . . .
and Completion**
82–87

Chapter 11
Going Public
88–97

Chapter 12
**The Great Man
of Science**
98–107

Chapter 13
The Widening Influence
108–115

Chapter 14
Darwin's Legacy Today
116–121

Timeline 122–123
Bibliography 124
For Further Study 125
Index 126–127

A Most Unusual Voyage

In December 1831, 22-year-old Charles Darwin stood at the rail of HMS *Beagle*, fighting seasickness and watching the English shoreline slide beneath the horizon. This round-the-world voyage was scheduled to last two years, but it would be nearly five before he saw England again.

In September 1835, the *Beagle* dropped anchor off one of the Galapagos Islands. As the landing party stepped ashore, they were struck by the otherworldly look of the island. The sun-baked lava rock and black sand blistered their feet, even through heavy boots.

At first Darwin was disappointed in the sparse plant and animal life. There were few mammals, and none larger than a rat. The plants, he wrote, were "wretched-looking little weeds." But soon the strangeness of the Galapagos began to work its magic. The Englishmen encountered dozens of giant 200-pound tortoises. Darwin gently brushed a hawk off a branch with the butt of his rifle and the bird did not bother to fly away. And he watched penguins sporting in the tropical waters—even though penguins were supposed to live only in the frozen reaches of Antarctica.

Darwin had signed on as the *Beagle*'s naturalist. He had always been an avid collector of fossils, insects, birds, and shells. During the voyage, he collected crates of specimens,

filled more than 20 books of notes, and trained himself as a scientist.

He also had immense curiosity. He wanted answers to the countless questions he encountered, and no place provided more questions than the Galapagos. Why were the creatures very much like animal life on the mainland of South America, but different enough to be separate species? Where did these differences come from? How were new species created? The Bible said that all plants and animals were created by God. Did he dare to think that the Bible story of creation might be wrong?

The *Beagle* was built for the British navy in 1820, and was later refitted for exploration.

Darwin could not get these questions out of his mind as the *Beagle* headed homeward. In the years that followed, he spent more and more time pondering what he called "that mystery of mysteries—the first appearance of new beings on this earth."

Eventually, he would develop a theory of evolution that would shake the scientific world—and society at large—more than any other before or since. And he would wait 20 years to publish it.

chapter 1

"A Very Ordinary Boy"

Servants moved with quiet efficiency through the halls of the Mount, the stately home of the Darwin family just outside London. On this morning of February 12, 1809, everyone on the staff was smiling about the good news that a son had been born to Susannah Wedgwood Darwin and Dr. Robert Darwin. The other Darwin children—three girls and a boy—raced around the spacious rooms, barely able to contain their excitement.

Charles Darwin grew up in comfortable middle class surroundings. While English society did not yet enjoy the

Built by Robert Darwin in 1800, the Mount overlooked the town of Shrewsbury.

use of inventions—such as washing machines and vacuum cleaners—that would be developed over the next 100 years, families like the Darwins did not suffer from the lack of labor-saving devices, for their small army of servants took care of every need. Charles was also fortunate to have three older sisters—Marianne, Caroline, and Susan—who smothered him with affection, especially after the death of their mother when Charles was eight. In most respects, Darwin's boyhood years were idyllic.

Darwin's most distinct memory of his mother was "her death-bed, her black velvet gown, and her curiously constructed work-table."

Still, throughout his life Darwin was troubled by the fact that he remembered almost nothing about his mother. His father, Dr. Robert, had something to do with that. Charles dearly loved his father, but he was also in awe of this huge 325-pound man whose powerful presence could make grown men quake. Dr. Robert was devastated by his wife's death, and wept often and openly in the weeks and months that followed. Family members commented that he was often moody and irritable. Charles's older sisters shared this prolonged grief, and they never talked about their mother in his presence. One of the Wedgwoods wrote that "the atmosphere at the Mount was one of never-ending gloom." It seems likely that Charles never understood much about

his mother's illness or her passing, and he would have been reluctant to break into the sadness of his father or his sisters to ask questions. No wonder his few memories faded!

Charles did not go to school until he was nine. Before that he was tutored at home, mostly by his older sister Caroline. In 1818, a year after Susannah Darwin's death, his father packed him off to Shrewsbury Grammar School, only about a mile from the Mount. Charles's older brother, Erasmus, known as "Ras," was already a student at the school and was able to help Charles over some of the rougher spots. The school was so dominated by its headmaster, Dr. Samuel Butler, that it became known as "Dr. Butler's School." He was a strict disciplinarian, determined to transform all his boys into scholars of the classics—well versed in Greek and Latin, but little else. To make matters worse, Charles was forced to board at the school, even though he could practically see his home from the campus. Years later he wrote in his autobiography, "Nothing could have been worse for the development of my mind than Dr. Butler's school…as a means of education to me

This portrait of Charles and his younger sister, Catherine, was painted when he was seven years old.

[it] was simply a blank."

To escape the school environment, Charles often sneaked out and ran home, racing back before the school was locked for the night. The comforts of home meant a great deal to him, and he felt most fortunate in being nurtured by not one family but two—the Darwins and his mother's family, the Wedgwoods.

Erasmus Darwin's most enduring contribution to science was his biology volume, *Zoonomia*.

The uniting of the two families had begun a generation earlier through the friendship of Charles's two grandfathers, Dr. Erasmus Darwin and Josiah Wedgwood. Erasmus Darwin was one of the most successful physicians in England. In fact, King George III had asked him to be his personal physician, but Dr. Darwin had refused. Like his son Robert, Erasmus was an enormous man—so huge that he had part of a table cut away for easier dining. He was also something of an inventor, with grand ideas for using steam engines to power road vehicles and flying machines long before either of these would come to be.

Erasmus Darwin gained even more fame for his own rather fanciful ideas about evolution. The famous poet Samuel Taylor Coleridge coined the term "darwinising" to describe the doctor's often wild theorizing. And by

Wedgwood Pottery

Josiah Wedgwood was a creative potter with a shrewd business sense. He offered classical shapes at affordable prices, and his ware was popular with the queen. His company became the world's largest pottery producer and still makes its delicate pieces today.

coincidence, Erasmus felt most comfortable writing in poetry. One long poem titled "The Temple of Nature" contained his musings about the formation of life, upon which his grandson would later build:

Organic life beneath the shoreless waves
Was born and nurs'd in ocean's pearly caves…

Erasmus's theories were rapidly discarded by scientists in the 19th century. But nevertheless, he did manage one practical invention—applying steam power to the pottery works of his friend Josiah Wedgwood.

The two friends often talked about how their families might be more closely united through the marriage of their offspring. It came to pass in 1796 when Susannah, Charles's mother and Josiah's daughter, accepted the proposal of Erasmus's son Robert. The unity of the two families would later be cemented by other Darwin-Wedgwood weddings.

Throughout his school years, Charles made the most of being a part of both families. He enjoyed long visits to Maer, the estate of his uncle, Josiah Wedgwood the younger. "I had a strong taste for angling [fishing]," he later recalled, "and would sit for any number of hours on the bank of a river or pond." And, encouraged by his father, he "became passionately fond of shooting." That passion included hunting. "I do not believe that anyone could have shown more zeal for the most holy cause than I did for shooting birds." That confession might sound inhumane to modern readers, but in the early 19th century, bird-shooting parties on wealthy estates were a standard component of the good life. Young Charles's marksmanship was considered an excellent credential for acceptance among England's wealthy landowners.

Charles struggled through seven years at Shrewsbury Grammar School, and although he was not achieving much in school, he was following his own path to intellectual growth. "I had strong and diversified tastes," he later recalled, "much zeal for whatever interested me, and a keen pleasure in understanding any complex subject or thing." He took such pleasure in geometry, and in reading the plays of Shakespeare and the works of poet Lord Byron and novelist Sir Walter Scott. He also enthusiastically collected minerals and insects, and enjoyed "watching the habits of birds, and even made notes on the subject." In another extracurricular activity, Charles helped Ras set up a chemistry laboratory

in a garden shed. "This was the best part of my education at school," he wrote, "for it showed me practically the meaning of experimental science." Dr. Butler, however, had not been impressed and publicly criticized the boys for wasting their time on a useless subject like chemistry.

The relationship between Charles and his father was complicated. Charles remembered his father as "the kindest man I ever knew," although Dr. Robert sometimes became angry over his son's tendency to march to his own drummer. In one outburst that Darwin never forgot, Dr. Robert shouted, "You care for nothing but shooting, dogs, and rat-catching, and you will be a disgrace to yourself and all your family."

Finally Dr. Robert acknowledged that Dr. Butler's school was not doing much for Charles, and decided to send him to Scotland's Edinburgh University to study medicine. His brother, Ras, was already finishing his second year there. Charles was delighted to be leaving Butler's, and was keenly aware that he had not been much of

The skilled Dr. Robert began practicing medicine at 20 years old, and had more than 50 patients within six months.

a scholar. "When I left the school," he wrote later, "I was for my age neither high nor low in it; and I believe that I was considered by all my masters and by my Father as a very ordinary boy, rather below the common standard in intellect."

In autumn 1825, Darwin headed to Scotland. He was thrilled to be reunited with his brother and excited by the bustling city. He bought armloads of books and signed up for as many courses as he was allowed.

But Darwin's enthusiasm did not last. The lectures bored him, and witnessing two surgeries made him sick. "The two cases fairly haunted me for many a long year," he wrote. Then, from conversations with Ras, Darwin learned that his father planned to leave him enough property to live comfortably. The awareness that he would not have to earn a living was enough to stop Darwin from making any strenuous effort to learn medicine.

Surgery in the 1820s

Medical science was still primitive in the early 1800s, and surgeries were performed without anesthesia. This meant that the patient was fully awake as a scalpel sliced through his flesh or a surgical saw ripped into his bone. The screams of a young boy undergoing surgery caused Charles Darwin to flee the room, and he eventually gave up any thoughts of a career in medicine.

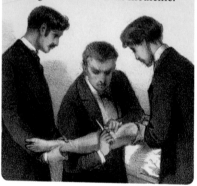

chapter 2

The Search for Direction

Darwin's time spent at Edinburgh was made tolerable by the presence of his brother and by his growing interest in natural history. He had enjoyed collecting natural specimens throughout his boyhood and, at Edinburgh, he devoted more time to exploring nature than to studying medicine. He spent hours examining the stuffed birds in the university's museum of natural history and went to a demonstration of bird taxidermy given by John James Audubon, the famous American naturalist and artist. Increasingly fascinated by the study of birds, he even learned taxidermy from a neighbor named John Edmonstone. Edmonstone, a former slave, may have been the only black man in Edinburgh.

This is Darwin's class card from Edinburgh University. Alexander Graham Bell, who invented the telephone, and Sir Arthur Conan Doyle, author of the famous Sherlock Holmes stories, also attended the university.

TAXIDERMY

The art of stuffing an animal skin and mounting it in a way that looks lifelike.

Darwin also joined the Plinian Society, a student club dedicated to discussing new developments in science. He

made a number of friends, including a faculty member named Robert Grant, who invited him on walks along the shore to search for unusual wildlife. Darwin sometimes joined fishermen in their boats, cheerfully poking through the muck on the decks to look for tiny sea creatures.

During his second year at Edinburgh, Darwin rarely went to the medical lectures. Not only had he lost interest in medicine, but life wasn't as much fun after his brother finished his schooling and left. For a few months, Ras went through the motions of being a physician. But he quickly tired of doctoring, moved to London, and settled into the life of a gentleman. In British society, young men of wealth could spend their time in pleasant idleness. They joined clubs, attended dinner parties, went fishing or hunting in the country, and traveled abroad. People saw nothing wrong in a man like Ras being perpetually unemployed. This was regarded as one of the privileges of wealth and social position, especially for the oldest son. However, Dr. Robert had no intention of supporting two sons in idleness.

As the summer of 1827 approached, Darwin

Ras and Charles were close throughout their lives, although the elder never developed any real professional interests.

searched for a way to tell his father he was not going to finish medical school. Dr. Robert, **Darwin's rooms at Christ's College had once been occupied by the great natural theologian William Paley. Both men's portraits now hang in the hallway of the college.**

who paid the bills, seemed to have figured that out already, but Darwin didn't know that. So, to avoid the inevitable confrontation he traveled instead of going home. He went to Ireland, then to London to check out his brother's bachelor lifestyle, but he found the city to be "a horrid smoky wilderness."

He also traveled to France with his uncle Josiah Wedgwood and two of his Wedgwood cousins. They spent several weeks in Paris, where Darwin seems to have spent much of the time with his cousin Emma. They were both

eighteen now and, as he wrote to his sisters, he was struck by how beautiful she had become. There were no signs of a romance, however, and Darwin finally decided to go back home and face his father.

No real confrontation occurred at the Mount because Dr. Robert had already decided what his son was going to do. Since a medical career was out, Darwin would have to enter the ministry. The Church of England provided a comfortable and respected position, especially for the younger sons of wealthy families. Charles readily agreed. He was not a particularly religious man, but he could picture himself preaching in a small village church, spending his free time wandering the fields and woods. Besides, almost any career was preferable to more medical lectures. One of his few regrets on leaving Edinburgh was that he never learned the skill of dissecting a specimen. This failure, along with an inability to draw, would haunt him throughout his career.

To become a minister, Darwin would have to study for three years at Christ's College, part of Cambridge University. He was willing to do this, but he was shocked to learn that the college required entering students to be fluent in classical Greek and Latin. Darwin had long since forgotten the small bits he had struggled to memorize at Dr. Butler's, so he was now faced with starting over. His father hired a tutor, and Darwin did his best to cram enough of the classical languages into his head to get through the tests. He eased the suffering by spending a lot of time with his sisters' friend

Fanny Owen, widely regarded as the most beautiful young woman in Shrewsbury. Finally, in January 1828, after eight months of grueling study, Darwin had passed all his exams and was off to Cambridge.

He spent three years at Cambridge and later wrote in his autobiography, "Upon the whole, the three years…were the most joyful in my happy life; I was then in excellent health, and almost always in high spirits." He quickly fell in with what he called a "sporting set," a group of young men from wealthy families who enjoyed hunting, riding, and partying far more than attending lectures. "We used often to dine together in the evening…," he confessed, "and sometimes we drank too much, with jolly singing and playing at cards afterwards." Still, Darwin's biographers agree that his student life was not really very wild—and he and all four of his closest college friends would go on to distinguished careers.

Darwin's academic career at Cambridge can best be described as uneven. He was bored by most lecture courses and he struggled with some subjects. He wrote to a friend about his math course, "I stick fast in the mud at the bottom [of the class] and there I shall remain."

One of the few classes he enjoyed was botany (the study of plants), taught by John Stevens

"Upon the whole, the three years I spent at Cambridge were the most joyful of my happy life."

–Charles Darwin, in a letter to a friend

Henslow. In addition to delivering interesting lectures, Henslow employed unusual techniques, such as taking his students on long trips by coach or river barge, and encouraging them to observe with an eye for scientific detail. Darwin became his favorite student. He dined often with the professor's family and went with Henslow on long walks through the Cambridge countryside—some faculty members even referred to Darwin as "the man who walks with Henslow." The botanist was also to play a major role in the upcoming drama of the *Beagle*.

Being part of the "sporting set" at Cambridge called for well-tailored clothes, such as the hunting jacket above.

Given Darwin's obsession with insects, one can imagine how thrilled he was when England was swept by a craze for collecting beetles. People competed to create the biggest or best collection and to find rare, or never-before-recorded species. Darwin found a beetle-chasing companion in his

cousin, William Darwin Fox, a fellow student at Cambridge. The two cousins seized every opportunity to go searching together, peeling the bark off fallen trees, turning over rocks so they could pounce on the exposed little creatures, and even hiring a local worker to help—until they discovered that the man was selling the best specimens to a wealthy collector.

On one "beetling" expedition, Darwin was holding a squirming beetle in each hand when he spotted a third, even more desirable, specimen. Intent on saving all three for his collection, he popped one of the beetles into his mouth. "Alas," he recalled, "it ejected some intensely acrid fluid, which burnt my tongue so that I was forced to spit the beetle out, which was lost, as well as the third one," which he never had a chance to pick up.

On occasion Darwin had the thrill of reporting a

"Go it Charlie!" is the caption for this cartoon, drawn by a friend, showing Darwin riding a gigantic beetle.

Go it Charlie !

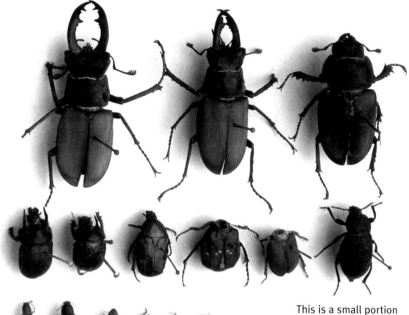

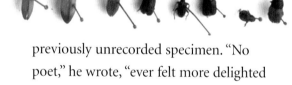

This is a small portion of Darwin's college beetle collection. His meticulous scholarship showed even then, in the very precise notes he kept on how the beetles differed from one another.

previously unrecorded specimen. "No poet," he wrote, "ever felt more delighted at seeing his first poem published than I did at seeing, in Stephens' 'Illustrations of British Insects,' the magic words, 'captured by C. Darwin, Esq.'"

Henslow was one of two faculty member who had strong influence on Darwin; the other was Adam Sedgwick, one of England's leading geologists. Through accompanying Sedgwick on geological surveys, Darwin learned that science involved more than the recording of facts; it was also essential to find patterns of meaning. "Nothing

GEOLOGY

Geology is the study of the earth's structure.

23

before," he wrote, "had ever made me thoroughly realize…
that science consists in grouping facts so that general laws or
conclusions may be drawn from them."

Henslow had taught Darwin to observe like a scientist,
while Sedgwick modeled the importance of developing
theories to make sense of the collected facts. These skills,
along with his great love of nature and ability to focus on its
tiniest details, would soon combine to guide Darwin on a
path that would change science—and the world—forever.

In the meantime, after struggling through one final set of
exams (with a good deal of cramming), Darwin completed
his Cambridge degree in 1831. Just before spring graduation
he read a book by Alexander von Humboldt, in which the
famed German naturalist and explorer
described his travels in South America.
The book was a fantastic combination
of adventure and scientific writing,
and it stirred in Darwin "a burning
zeal to add even the most
humble contribution to
the noble structure of
Natural Science."
During the

Adam Sedgwick is often called
the "father of geology." He was
a spellbinding speaker, and
opened his lectures to women,
which was quite rare in the
mid-1800s.

summer, while on a geological expedition to northern Wales with Sedgwick, Darwin began making his plans. He would spend time with his family at the Mount, take part in the autumn hunting, then make an excursion to see the natural wonders of the Canary Islands. His career in the ministry could wait a few months.

Darwin arrived home on August 29, 1831, to find a letter waiting for him—a letter destined to change the course of his life.

Humboldt and Popular Science

Baron Alexander von Humboldt (1769–1859) was an outstanding nature writer—and a prolific one. His words painted vivid pictures of exotic locales in South America, Asia, and scores of tropical islands. In the early 1800s, there was a growing hunger for information about such places, as well as about the plants and animals living there. To satisfy their curiosity, people eagerly read detailed scientific works such as Humboldt's. They also pored over drawings and paintings, and attended long public lectures on these fascinating topics and far away lands.

The volcanoes and rock structures of the Canary Islands have long made them a popular destination for naturalists.

chapter 3

Signing On

"The voyage of the *Beagle*," Darwin later wrote, "has been by far the most important event in my life, and has determined my whole career." But this historic voyage almost didn't happen. Everything depended, he explained, "on so small a circumstance as my uncle offering to drive me thirty miles to Shrewsbury, which few uncles would have done, and on such a trifle as the shape of my nose." Here is how these improbable events unfolded:

The letter Darwin received when he returned home from Wales was from Henslow, his Cambridge botany professor. It contained the remarkable offer of a position as the unpaid naturalist on HMS *Beagle*, which would soon depart to make coastal surveys of South America and then return to England by way of the Pacific and Indian Oceans. Henslow explained that Robert FitzRoy, the ship's captain, was primarily interested in an "amiable companion" who would share his interest in natural history. It seemed that FitzRoy, a member of an upper class family, did not feel comfortable socializing with the junior officers.

HMS
The initials HMS stand for His (or Her) Majesty's Ship.

Henslow had been asked to name a likely candidate and, of course, he had suggested Darwin. Would Charles accept the offer?

Darwin immediately wrote a response, happily accepting. But the next morning his dream was shattered when his father angrily refused to approve what he called a "wild scheme." It struck Dr. Robert as one more instance of Charles changing professions. And, after so much wandering, how would he ever settle down to the life of a clergyman?

Darwin was crushed. He could not defy his father and, even if he did, he had no money of his own to pay his expenses for a two- or three-year voyage. Hiding his disappointment,

The *Beagle's* Mission

One of the nagging problems of ship navigation was determining longitude. After dedicating his entire working life to the problem, Englishman John Harrison invented a chronometer that allowed navigators to accurately tell time at sea, and thus determine longitude anywhere in the world. One of FitzRoy's tasks was to test a variety of these devices at different locations on the *Beagle's* voyage.

he wrote another letter, this time turning down the offer, adding, "But if it had not been for my father, I would have taken all risks."

On August 31, a deflated Darwin rode to Maer, the Wedgwood estate, to take part in some September partridge hunting. He always felt more relaxed and comfortable with

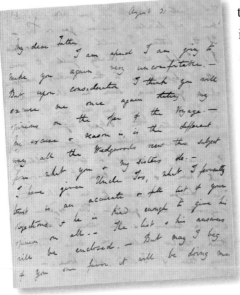

the Wedgwoods than in the more controlled atmosphere of the Mount, so he felt at ease explaining his disappointment to his uncle and cousins. All of the Wedgwoods were horrified at Dr. Robert's refusal, especially since the offer sounded so perfect for Charles.

This is the first page of Darwin's letter, the full text of which appears on the opposite page.

Fortunately, Darwin also told the Wedgwoods that his father had left one loophole by saying, "If you can find any man of common-sense who advises you to go, I will give my consent." That was the only opening Uncle Josiah needed. He immediately had Darwin write down each of his father's objections to the venture. Uncle Jos, as Darwin called him, then wrote a letter to his brother-in-law, giving his answer to each objection. He argued that the voyage was not incompatible with becoming a minister; in fact, he wrote, "the pursuit of Natural History is very suitable to a clergyman." And, since Charles would be studying natural history at home anyhow, he would not really be changing professions. He wisely concluded by saying he recognized

that "you and Charles are the persons who must decide."

Darwin then penned an apologetic letter to his father. As the excerpts below indicate, he was most unwilling to go against Dr. Robert in spite of his burning desire to sail on the *Beagle*:

Maer August 31st, 1831

My dear Father,

I am afraid I am going to make you again very uncomfortable—but upon consideration I think you will excuse me once again stating my opinions on the offer of the voyage. My excuse and reason is the different way all the Wedgwoods view the subject from what you and my sisters do. I have given Uncle Jos, what I fervently trust is an accurate and full list of your objections, and he is kind enough to give his opinion on all. The list and his answers will be enclosed, but may I beg you one favour, it will be doing me the greatest kindness if you will send me a decided answer—Yes or No; If the latter…[I will] yield to your better judgment and to the kindest indulgence which you have shown me all through my life,—and you may rely upon it I will never mention the subject again. …I do not know what to say about Uncle Jos's kindness, I never can forget how he interests himself about me.

Believe me, my dear Father,
Your affectionate son,

Charles Darwin

The next morning, with his hopes rekindled, Darwin took his dog and gun and went hunting. He had not gone far before a Wedgwood servant caught up with him and led him back to the house. Uncle Jos, it turned out, was not satisfied with having the letters delivered. The only solution was for them both to drive the nearly thirty miles to Shrewsbury and meet with Dr. Robert at the Mount.

Charles was a bundle of nerves as they approached his house. He could hardly catch his breath, but the meeting went well. Dr. Robert yielded on point after point and even became jovial. When discussing the expenses of the journey, Charles commented, "I would have to be deuced clever to spend much money aboard ship." His father answered, "But they tell me you are very clever." The doctor then graciously gave his consent.

Darwin was now in a near panic to settle the matter before it was too late. He quickly wrote a letter reversing his earlier refusal and saying he would be "very happy to have the honour of accepting." Unable to sleep, he took the 3 a.m. express coach to Cambridge. As soon as he arrived, Henslow met him with more bad news: Apparently Captain FitzRoy was considering taking another naturalist,

Darwin would come to admire FitzRoy's noble character, despite the captain's bouts of temper and melancholy.

his friend Mr. Chester. Once again, Darwin was devastated and Henslow had difficulty persuading him to go to London and meet with FitzRoy. The captain of the *Beagle* had not canceled the interview, so there was still a chance of success.

On September 5, 1831, Darwin went to London and met with FitzRoy. He was instantly relieved to learn that Mr. Chester was unable to leave England, so he was out of the picture—and everything depended on the result of this meeting. But early in the conversation, Darwin sensed something

The *Beagle* Brig

In the early 1800s, the British had taken the lead in trying to end the slave trade, arguing that it was morally wrong. Most of their existing ships were too large and slow to catch the speedy craft used by slavers, however, so the Royal Navy designed a swifter brig class, of which the *Beagle* was a part. But when ten guns were added to the brigs' design, the ships had a tendency to roll over, leading to the nickname the "coffin-brig class." By 1831, ship designers claimed to have fixed the problem—and by the time of Darwin's voyage, the *Beagle* had already survived one surveying trip to South America—but the nickname still caused him a little uneasiness!

was not quite right. Only later did he learn that, as soon as he had entered the room, FitzRoy had been troubled by the shape of his nose! The captain believed in a strange "science" which held that a person's character could be determined by his facial characteristics. FitzRoy worried that a man with a nose like Darwin's would not be able to withstand the hardships of an around-the-world voyage.

31

Although Darwin was not certain what the trouble was, he sensed that it was important to show that he could face any danger or difficulty. He did everything he could to show his enthusiasm for the voyage, and eventually convinced FitzRoy that he was right for the naturalist job. For his part, Darwin was quite enchanted by the *Beagle*'s captain. FitzRoy's manners were very aristocratic, which seemed natural since he was a descendant of King Charles II. His character, Darwin noted, had many noble qualities: He was brave, determined, devoted to his work, and seemed extremely generous and a friend to all. Thus, the matter was settled, and Darwin was told to get ready to sail in a matter of weeks.

All of London was decked out for a celebration in those early days of September 1831, not because of Darwin's signing on to

The coronation of King William IV took place at London's Westminster Abbey, and displayed the color and elegance of 19th-century England.

HMS *Beagle*, but to celebrate the coronation of King William IV and Queen Adelaide. All the shops were closed and the city was decorated with flags and gas lights. Since he could not start making necessary purchases, Darwin bought a seat to watch the procession and the fireworks. Then he wrote an urgent letter to his sister:

> *My Dear Susan—Again I am going to trouble you. I suspect, if I keep on at this rate, you will sincerely wish me at Tierra del Fuego, [or anywhere] but England. First, tell Nancy to make me twelve instead of eight shirts. Tell Edward to send me up in my carpet-bag…my slippers, a pair of lightish walking-shoes, my Spanish books, my new microscope…a little book, if I have it in my bedroom—[on] Taxidermy.*

Darwin was in excellent shape for the grueling journey that lay ahead. As a boy he could high jump over a bar set at his shoulder height, and hunting, riding, and long nature hikes had kept him in good condition. At the age of 22, he stood about six feet tall, and had a fairly athletic build. He also had the self-confidence of a wealthy English gentleman, accustomed to being addressed as "Sir," and comfortable dressed in an elegant waistcoat and top hat, even when strolling the countryside. Darwin made friends easily and seems to have been well liked by everyone who knew him. As a Cambridge friend said, even at large parties of 50 or 60 people, "he was ever one of the most cheerful, most popular, and most welcome."

4

The Voyage of the *Beagle* Begins

In mid-September 1831, Darwin and Captain FitzRoy traveled to Plymouth to look over their ship, but they were disappointed to find the work crews woefully behind schedule. More delays followed, and Darwin later called the weeks of uncertainty the "most miserable" of his life.

He was also stunned by HMS *Beagle*'s small size. The ship was only 90 feet (27 m) long, so there was little space for 74 men, along with their gear, food, supplies, 10 cannons, and 22 chronometers. Darwin found that he would be sharing a cabin with another man and would be sleeping in a hammock hung over the chart table. He could make room for his feet only by removing two drawers from a cabinet.

In spite of the frustrations, he found much that was exciting. "No vessel has been fitted out so expensively and with so much care," he wrote. "Everything that can be is made of mahogany." And, as the departure time drew closer, his excitement increased. In a note to FitzRoy he declared that the voyage would be like "a birthday for the rest of my life."

On December 27, 1831, HMS *Beagle* finally put out to sea, riding the billowing waves of the Atlantic Ocean. But Charles Darwin did not enjoy a moment of it! Instead, he became

violently seasick. Day after day he lay in his hammock, often too weak to stand and too sick to eat anything but a few

raisins prescribed by his father. He was also disappointed when the ship's first planned stop, the Canary Islands (the goal of Darwin's Cambridge travel dreams), was abandoned because rumors of a cholera epidemic would have made a two-week quarantine necessary before they could land.

The crew sailed on to the Cape Verde Islands off the coast of Africa, and from this point on, the voyage changed dramatically for Darwin. He had his first view of a tropical rain forest, which he described as "a glorious day, like giving sight to a blind man's eyes."

After allowing three weeks for

The *Beagle* was roughly the length of the distance between bases on a baseball diamond.

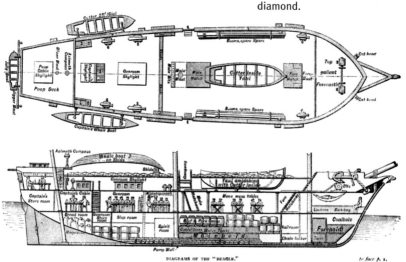

DIAGRAMS OF THE "BEAGLE."

FitzRoy to chart the islands, the *Beagle* sailed west for Brazil. Once they crossed the equator, the seas calmed and Darwin began to feel better. They arrived at the coast of Brazil in February 1832 and, for the next two years, Captain FitzRoy worked the *Beagle* up and down the east coast of South America. For roughly two-thirds of that time, Darwin was able to stay on land, often for two or three months at a time.

He became an eager collector of everything on land and at sea—insects, birds, animals, fossils, sea creatures, shells, bones. He filled book after book with notes, in addition to a daily diary. His writing became detailed and colorful, with an engaging style. His first description of a Brazilian rain forest is a good illustration of his ability to record the vividness of his experiences: "The delight one experiences in such times bewilders the

This painting by Augustus Earle captures the majesty of the Brazilian landscape that so impressed Darwin.

mind. If the eye attempts to follow the flight of a gaudy butterfly, it is arrested by some strange tree or fruit; if watching an insect one forgets it in the stranger flower it is crawling over."

Darwin was in his glory. Every moment of every day was filled with new adventures. When he was on board the *Beagle*, his appearance must have made an unusual impression on the others. Most of the men were in uniform, including 34 seamen and eight marines, as well as the ship's junior officers, two mates, and the captain. Darwin, by contrast, normally wore a topcoat with tails, a waistcoat, a high-collared shirt, and a cravat (tie)—the standard outfit of a 19th century English gentleman.

Despite Darwin's aristocratic clothing, the crew quickly became very fond of him. They referred to him as "our flycatcher," and were impressed by his immense energy, fearlessness, and kindness. One officer, James Sullivan, recalled:

Augustus Earle (1793–1838)

As official artist, Augustus Earle was a vital member of the *Beagle* crew. Artists were essential on every journey of exploration—they created the only visual record for those back home, as photographers would do later. Through his worldwide travels, Earle recorded through watercolor and pencil sketches the landscapes and people he encountered, always in colorful detail. Darwin and Earle got along so well that they rented a house in Brazil together when there was a chance to leave the ship for several weeks. Like Darwin, the artist was fearless and adventuresome until ill-health forced him to return to England. He was then replaced by another outstanding artist, Conrad Martens.

"I can confidently express my belief that during the five years in the *Beagle*, he was never known to be out of temper, or to say one unkind or hasty word [about] or to anyone...."

Darwin's relationship with FitzRoy was more complex. He was constantly impressed by the captain's skills as a navigator and a leader. "I feel nothing is too great or too high for him," Darwin wrote. "Altogether he is the strongest...character I ever fell in with." But no one knew that FitzRoy was suffering from severe psychological problems until they began to show in violent outbursts. Darwin first encountered one of these episodes when he told FitzRoy of his outrage at seeing a slave auction in Brazil. When FitzRoy defended slavery, the two men argued; then FitzRoy exploded and ordered Darwin to leave his ship—for good. Fortunately, the *Beagle*'s captain apologized and the incident was soon over, if not forgotten. At one time or another, everyone on the ship experienced FitzRoy's rage, but it may have been

This gaucho catches a rhea with a *bola*, a weighted rope that entangles itself in the bird's legs. His loose-fitting pants and bulky cloth belt are typical gaucho garb.

Darwin collected specimens of wildlife never before cataloged, including the Patagonian cavy and a small ostrichlike bird, now called "Darwin's rhea."

worse for Darwin because he dared to stand up to the captain. Still, most of the time, FitzRoy did what he could to help Darwin, and he increasingly admired the naturalist for his energy and courage.

After the ship sailed south to Argentina, Darwin experienced some of the most remarkable adventures of the entire voyage. The land was flatter and drier than Brazil, much of it covered by the prairie region called the Pampas. This was a wild grassland where hard-riding Argentinian cowboys—the *gauchos*—herded cattle on the open range.

Darwin was fascinated by the gauchos and he rode with them for several weeks. He shared their rugged way of life, covering 600 miles (960 km) on horseback, eating nothing but wild meat and a few ostrich eggs, and sleeping on the ground around a campfire. Armed with his rifle and with two pistols stuck in his belt, Darwin seemed to relish the danger. Along the way, he encountered bandits and native warriors, and barely escaped the shooting at the start of two uprisings!

Fortunately, these adventures did not prevent Darwin from collecting crates of specimens and filling notebooks with observations and notes.

39

Mail At Sea

There was no official postal service in the 1830s. People at sea would leave mail and packages with any ship they encountered that might be able to carry their package or letter to the right person. Because HMS *Beagle* was a government-owned ship, Darwin and the crew relied heavily on British warships. Apparently none of Darwin's letters or crates of specimens was lost.

He even trained one of the ship's boys, Syms Covington, to assist him with the collecting, adding greatly to the mounds of material that cluttered the deck of the *Beagle*. Whenever they encountered a ship headed for England, Darwin and Covington packed crates with specimens for shipment to Henslow, along with Darwin's long, descriptive letters written in his lively prose. He did not yet know that Henslow was reporting his findings to fascinated scientific gatherings in Cambridge and London. While Darwin was on the far side of the world, he was becoming a well-known scientist back home.

Many of Darwin's reports involved geological finds, such as the amazing discoveries he made in Argentina. At a place called Punta Alta, he spotted fossilized bones in a mound of clay and gravel. As he began digging them out he found that all of the bones were remarkably large—the remains of huge creatures that had long ago become extinct and were unknown to 19th-century scientists. What was most striking to Darwin

was that some of these creatures were similar to more modern animals. For example, although the extinct giant sloth was as large as a hippopotamus, it still had bone patterns similar to much-smaller modern sloths. Other bones suggested an elephantlike creature; another unusual find was a prehistoric form of horse.

The fossils turned out to be among Darwin's most important discoveries. Few people in the 1830s were aware of fossils; fewer still had any idea what they were—the first fossils of dinosaurs had been dug up in 1822. As more dinosaur fossils were found, people became increasingly fascinated, but still didn't know what to make of them. Many believed the bones were from strange creatures that had been destroyed in the great flood described in the Bible. The giant fossils Darwin found in Argentina were viewed the same way. Captain FitzRoy, for example, was one of many who believed that creatures like mastodons had become extinct because they were too large to get through the door of Noah's ark!

Darwin was most fascinated with the question of how the fossils he found of giant creatures were

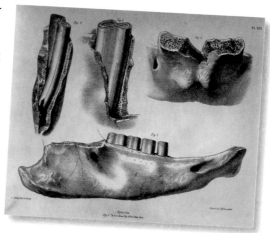

Darwin found these fossils of a mylodon, or giant ground sloth, on a Brazilian beach.

41

related to today's similar but smaller creatures. "This wonderful relationship," he wrote, "between the dead and the living will, I do not doubt, hereafter throw more light on the appearance of organic beings on earth and their disappearance from it." Could it be, he wondered, that life-forms were constantly changing and that some died out, while others continued to change and survive? It was a revolutionary idea and an exciting one. He knew he needed far more evidence to answer the questions swirling in his mind, but this pondering was his first step toward a theory of evolution.

The *Beagle's* next destination was the west coast of the continent. This involved passing through the treacherous seas around Tierra del Fuego, where narrow channels between rocky islands could spell disaster for ships trying to reach the Pacific Ocean. Several thousand Native Americans lived a hard, primitive life on these windswept

Here the *Beagle* sails a 150-mile (241 km) passageway between two islands off Tierra del Fuego, later named the Beagle Channel.

islands. On an earlier voyage, Captain FitzRoy had picked up three of these Fuegians and taken them to England, where they dressed in European clothes, learned the language, and met the king and queen. Now, with high hopes, he returned them to their islands, still dressed in finery and equipped with fine china and glassware.

Fuegian natives sometimes pirated passing ships. The *Beagle* was involved in one such skirmish.

Within days of the *Beagle*'s departure, the Fuegians shed their clothes and "civilized" ways. When the ship returned, FitzRoy was crushed to see that his experiment had failed. Darwin concluded that it was a mistake to try to force European civilization onto indigenous peoples. He felt it would be best to leave them alone, but he was also convinced that such native populations would soon enough be overwhelmed by Europeans and Americans, who were rapidly taking over native lands on every continent.

As the *Beagle* continued into the Pacific, Darwin again displayed his great courage. A landing party from the ship was nearly left stranded when a huge portion of a glacier broke loose and crashed into the sea, sending great waves over their boats and supplies. The men were on a high cliff and too far away to reach the boats in time, so Darwin made a dash into the pounding surf to save them. To honor this heroism, FitzRoy named a peak on Tierra del Fuego "Mount Darwin."

In June 1834, the *Beagle* sailed into the Pacific and up the west coast of South America. Darwin had recently received the renowned Charles Lyell's *Principles of Geology*, and he used the months that followed for lengthy geological trips into the towering Andes. He was fascinated to find an entire forest of petrified trees at an altitude of 12,000 feet (3,658 m), far above the 19th-century tree line and, later, a bed of fossilized seashells. How could trees grow so high, in such harsh conditions? How could there be seashells unless these lands were once covered by the sea? These questions were clear indications that the land had changed over time.

Darwin encountered more evidence of the changing earth when he witnessed volcanic eruptions, and when Chile was rocked by a massive earthquake and tidal wave on February 20, 1835. "The whole coast," he wrote, "is strewed over with timber and furniture as if a thousand ships had been wrecked."

These experiences and his speculation about fossils were leading Darwin to see all life, as well as the physical structure of the earth, as fluid and constantly changing. He could no longer accept the Bible's account of creation taking place in a few days.

Darwin's colorful cross-section of the Andes was used in his first book on geology.

After a year of charting Chile's coast, FitzRoy announced that it was time to sail west, across the Pacific and Indian Oceans. Darwin had now been living his life of adventure for more than three years. His body was toughened by the rugged lifestyle, and he had grown into an always-curious scientist with a keen eye for collecting and organizing evidence. In 1833 he wrote to his sister Catherine: "The pleasure of a first day's partridge shooting…cannot be compared to finding a group of fossil bones, which tell their story of former times with almost a living tongue." Darwin's delight in the natural world was now a full-fledged passion. The idea of going home to the life of a minister seemed increasingly unlikely.

"In the Beginning ..."

In the early 1800s, most people believed the Bible's account of creation. By adding up the life spans in Genesis, a 17th-century archbishop even deduced an exact date: 4004 BC. But by Darwin's time, a few scholars had begun to question this literal interpretation. Charles Lyell wrote that landforms had changed over time, and zoologist Jean-Baptiste Lamarck and Erasmus Darwin both wrote of changing lifeforms. They gave no hint of *how* these changes occurred, however, so their ideas were largely ignored by the public.

chapter **5**

The *Beagle* in the Galapagos

On September 15, 1835, HMS *Beagle* arrived at the Galapagos, a small group of islands almost 600 miles west of Ecuador. The ship remained for barely a month, and the men were happy to leave. For them the islands were little more than a rather bizarre delay in the long journey home.

For Darwin, however, the Galapagos became something more—something incredibly important. In later years, it would seem as if the entire voyage—maybe even his entire life—had been destined to bring him to these

The odd plants and rock formations of the Galapagos made Darwin feel like he had sailed to another planet.